THE ALCESTIAD
With a Satyr Play
THE DRUNKEN SISTERS

A *Cass Canfield* BOOK

BOOKS BY THORNTON WILDER

NOVELS

The Cabala
The Bridge of San Luis Rey
The Woman of Andros
Heaven's My Destination
The Ides of March
The Eighth Day
Theophilus North

COLLECTIONS OF SHORT PLAYS

The Angel That Troubled the Waters
The Long Christmas Dinner

PLAYS

Our Town
The Merchant of Yonkers
The Skin of Our Teeth
The Alcestiad, *with a Satyr Play*,
The Drunken Sisters

COLLECTION OF LONG PLAYS

Three Plays:
Our Town
The Skin of Our Teeth
The Matchmaker

THORNTON WILDER

THE ALCESTIAD

OR

A Life in the Sun

A PLAY IN THREE ACTS

WITH A SATYR PLAY

THE DRUNKEN SISTERS

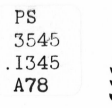

HARPER & ROW, PUBLISHERS

NEW YORK, HAGERSTOWN, SAN FRANCISCO

LONDON

The Drunken Sisters was published in the November 1957 issue of *The Atlantic.*

A limited edition of this book has been privately printed by The Franklin Library.

FIRST TRADE EDITION

Designed by Sidney Feinberg

Library of Congress Cataloging in Publication Data

Wilder, Thornton Niven, 1897–1975.
  The Alcestiad.
  (A Cass Canfield book)
  1. Alcestis—Drama. I. Wilder, Thornton Niven,
1897–1975. The drunken sisters. 1977. II. Title.
PS3545.I345A78   1977   812'.5'2   77–3781
ISBN 0–06–014638–9

---

77 78 79 80 10 9 8 7 6 5 4 3 2 1

Contents

Foreword

On the last pages of Thornton Wilder's novel *The Eighth Day*, my brother has one of the leading characters refute the usual image of the life experience as a river flowing onward between defined banks. Instead, the human adventure is described as a tapestry with indeterminate breadth as well as length and the individual pattern visible on both sides of the fabric. The story is outlined in colored yarn, the design perhaps wildly asymmetrical but nevertheless clear, truthful, complete. A record and a portrait.

Thornton's tapestry was minute when at the age of seven or eight in Madison, Wisconsin, he first heard the name Alcestis while reading or being read to from Bulfinch's *The Age of Fable*. The story of the daughter of King Pelias, princess of princesses in the myth and the song of pre-Christian Greece, captured his imagination—and his heart. The thread of her white yarn was knotted into his bit of fabric and she became a benign insistence in his inner consciousness, that hidden storehouse which is an author's source and springboard. She was the haunting shadow of a play that would take years to write.

The knot in Alcestis's thread was tied when the Wilder family moved to Berkeley, California, where the magnificent Greek Theater built into the hillside of a eucalyptus grove was a new and lively part of the life of the university and the town. Several times a year the Classics Department mounted productions of plays by Sophocles, Aeschylus, and Euripides. Our mother joined the volunteer workers in the costume shop and stenciled furlongs of borders in the Greek key or laurel leaf patterns on gorgeously colored togas. She made a little blue one with shells around the hem for Thornton—and a green one for brother Amos—and sent them off to apply for roles as members of the Athenean mob. Thus Thornton discovered "total" theater and the Golden Age of Antiquity. His experience until then had been a performance of *As You Like It* seen from the top gallery of a Milwaukee theater.

By now Thornton was ten; black-haired, blue-eyed, acquisitive and radiant. Even before this he had claimed his share of a writer's allotment of the twenty-six letters of the alphabet and had begun to tame them into a vocabulary that would allow him —in good time—to speak in his own way. He went to bed early and got up early to write, and the full range of his enlarging vocabulary was turned to inventing dialogue. He draped us and the neighbors' children in yards of begged or borrowed cheese-cloth and coaxed us into declaiming his grandiloquent speeches.

Four years later he was a boarding pupil in the China Inland Mission School in Chefoo. Studies in the classics began early in a British school preparing its pupils for the Oxford-Cambridge Examinations.

The first half of his undergraduate years was spent at Oberlin College in Ohio, where he became a privileged student and friend of a great teacher who was also a distinguished classicist—Professor Charles H. A. Wager. Alcestis's thread wove a visibly increasing pattern during these years and later, following his graduation from Yale in 1920, when he spent eight months at the American Academy for Classical Studies in Rome. Not qualified as a Graduate Fellow, he nevertheless audited lectures, went on digs with the archaeologists and pored over fragile papyri. In the museums and art galleries of Italy he caught Alcestis's shadow.

In the decades of the twenties and the thirties the tapestry grew in size and density. The design was of teaching—first French at The Lawrenceville School and then comparative literature, including the Greek dramatists, at the University of Chicago—and lecture tours and script-writing in Hollywood. He published two volumes of short plays and four novels. One, *The Bridge of San Luis Rey*, brought him the first of three Pulitzer Prizes and, at the age of thirty, world-wide fame weighted with a cumbersome bag of perquisites: honors, privileges, dazzling opportunities balanced by loss of privacy and hazards to body, mind, and spirit.

During these years the first of Thornton's long plays, *Our Town*, was produced to immediate success, and the second, *The Merchant of Yonkers*, to failure. André Obey's play, *Lucréce*, which Katharine Cornell had commissioned my brother to translate for her, opened and closed while Ibsen's *A Doll's House*, adapted by him for Ruth Gordon, was a conspicuous success.

In the summer of 1939 Thornton returned home wonderfully free at last of all outside commitments, with his head full of plans for his own work. He had the beginnings of two projects, both plays. One did not have a name yet. The other was *The Alcestiad*. September came and Hitler's armies flooded Holland and Belgium. Thornton had no choice; *The Alcestiad* was not a play for a war-torn world. The untitled project which became *The Skin of Our Teeth* was.

Soon after Pearl Harbor Thornton was commissioned a captain in the Air Force. By strange coincidence his final leave before going overseas came at the time of the previews and opening of *The Skin of Our Teeth* in New York. The morning that Mother and I said goodbye to him he patted his bulging duffle bag. "I have the manuscript of *The Alcestiad* in my kit. I've been thinking how I could make it into a good one-act. It's very possible by using just the big second act scene. I'd like to leave a finished piece of work . . . might come in handy, Mother. It's a toss-up if *The Skin of Our Teeth* will catch on. . . ."

Two years later, while he was waiting in a camp near Boston to be separated from the Air Force (a lieutenant colonel now), his papers were lost. The commanding officer of the post offered a three-day pass. Thornton went straight from the Back Bay station to the Boston Public Library on Copley Square, where he drowned himself once more in the Golden Age of Greece. A few days later he was for the first time in more than three years seated at his own desk in Hamden, Connecticut.

A single sheet of paper from that time is before me now. Printed on one side in big block letters is:

THE ALCESTIAD
A PLAY OF QUESTIONS

On the reverse in his small careful penmanship is:

(Sketches up to and including the Tiresias scene
of Act One had been made before the War and lost)
Draft One of the first act, May and July 1945
Draft Two, begun July 8, 1945
This Draft Three begun (after completion of Act II
and half of Act III) on Dec

The unfinished date would be 1945.

The loss of the manuscript meant more to my brother than these few notes convey; his eagerness to get back to his peacetime profession fired his enthusiasm and carried him along for the seven months of work recorded here. But, like millions of other soldiers, he had returned home not only a disoriented and exhausted man but a changed one. He was not able easily to recapture his prewar vision of Alcestis and he did not have the reserve of physical and nervous energy to sustain the excitement and tension to finish his work. He found he was beginning to destroy rather than build. Fortunately he recognized this and put the manuscript away again before doing it injury.

Ancient literature is replete with warriors and battlefields, tyrants and heroes. My brother's thoughts were still lively with his own recent experiences of Hitler's and Mussolini's wars: one year spent on the North African coast among the ruins and ghosts of Hellenic and Roman conquest; another year in southern Italy, likewise haunted by dramatic legend, with Caesar's image triumphant. Thornton suddenly saw his next work plain. And so it happened that the novel, *The Ides of March*, was written and published in 1948. It opened the way for his return to civilian life, to teaching and lecturing again, to the theater and to Alcestis.

Thornton was only one of many authors after Euripides to be inspired to retell in his own way the Alcestis fable. Among others Christoph Martin Wieland in Germany in 1773 wrote a libretto for an operetta on the subject. In the next century the poets Richard von Hofmannstahl in Austria and Robert Browning in England used the myth. T. S. Eliot borrowed from it for an aspect of his successful play, *The Cocktail Party*. And no wonder, for the theme of conjugal love and the willingness of a wife to die for her husband is an appealing and thought-provoking challenge to any author anxious to explore and praise the capabilities of humankind.

After the success at the 1954 Edinburgh Festival of *The Matchmaker*—that happy invention which started its career as the New York failure *The Merchant of Yonkers* and went on to become the basis of the musical comedy hit, *Hello, Dolly!*—the producers commissioned from my brother a new play for the next season. This gave him the impetus needed to finish *The Alcestiad*. He went into hiding at Aix-en-Provence for a long working period. At Christmas he joined a group of friends and me at Villars, Switzerland, for two weeks. During that time I typed from the manuscript the first two acts of the new text. He submitted them at once to the Festival Committee. They and Tyrone Guthrie accepted the play for their 1955 program. Before leaving Aix in the spring he sent in Act Three.

A performance of the Classic Attic theater consisted of a trilogy of more or less connected tragedies usually followed by a Satyr play—a humorous or biting comment using characters and situations from the preceding dramas. Euripides, the youngest of the three major rival playwrights, sometimes broke with tradition by writing a single play that could stand alone or be grouped with others to complete the three-part pattern. His *Alcestis* is one of these. In fact, because of its "happy ending," with the heroine brought back from the underworld by Hercules, *Alcestis* was even used occasionally as a Satyr play.

My brother's first idea for his version of the story was to commission a new translation of Euripides's text for a middle act and write a first and third to frame it. Soon he discarded the plan as not practical for his purposes.

In the Greek telling of the legend and Bulfinch's account centuries later, King Admetus knows that he can be saved from death if another will die for him. He goes begging the favor among his servants, former military colleagues, and friends to no avail. Next, he beseeches his parents relentlessly, pointing out that since they have so few years of living left, it is a little thing to ask. But neither the old father nor the old mother is willing to give up a breath for the son. The King does not request this sacrifice of his Queen; when Alcestis offers her life with all her love his protests seem mild and unworthy.

Thornton, by having Admetus unaware that he can be saved by another's death, gains a very dramatic and human emotional

peak in act two, and deepens the characterizations and relation-
ship of husband and wife, enriching the bare outlines of the
legend for our twentieth century understanding. Concerning his
version my brother has said:*

> On one level my play recounts the life of a woman—of many
> women—from bewildered bride to sorely tested wife to overbur-
> dened old age. On another level it is a wildly romantic story of gods
> and men, of death and hell, of resurrection of great loves and great
> trials, of usurpation and revenge. On another level, however, it is
> a comedy . . . about the extreme difficulty of any dialogue between
> heaven and earth, about the misunderstandings that result from the
> incommensurability of things human and divine.

Of Thornton's other works, his third novel, *The Woman of
Andros*, published in 1930, comes closest in setting, feeling, and
ideas to *The Alcestiad*. Laid on a small Grecian island when Alcestis was already a legend, it is a nostalgic, quiet yet passionate
prose-poem, a bridge with one end mired in the mud of the cruel
pagan world, the other straining toward a slowly rising dawn of
release. The heroine, Chrysis, is beautiful, intelligent, and has
some education, but her profession as a *heitara* makes her an
outcast. Nevertheless, she is spiritual sister to the Queen Alcestis.

In both these female characters Thornton pays his *hommage* to
all women, giving them the burden of carrying his message.
Chrysis in her living and her dying praises all life—"the bright
and the dark"—and teaches others to do likewise. She is unknow-
ingly a prophet, pointing ahead to a higher hope for humanity.

Alcestis, of course, had been entrusted with messages and
heaped with laurel wreaths long before Thornton heard her
name. In his play, brought back from hell to live again in the
Golden Light of Apollo, she is not permitted a human end. The

---

*Quoted by Paul M. Cubeta in *Modern Drama for Analysis* (New York: Holt,
Rinehart & Winston, Inc., 1955), pp. 595–596.

God steals her from Death and insists upon her perpetual life. He steals her from Admetus, thus denying her—and the king—a stela at his side in the royal tomb. Apollo leads her to His Evergreen Grove where she still wanders, a symbol, a myth, a truth for us all: one who escaped from darkness to be herself a light on the horizon comprehensible to the spirit of Christian humanism.

A play written in the form of ancient Greek drama should logically be performed in the traditional classic manner, in a setting of marble columns under a sun-lighted blue sky. Thornton wrote his *Alcestiad* so that it could be accommodated to the conventional theater of the proscenium arch. At Edinburgh it was presented under still other circumstances, in the vast barn of a building known as The Church of Scotland Assembly Hall, box-shaped with rows and rows of uncomfortable seats facing three directions—a perfect setting for stormy sessions of factions warring over church politics and church dogma.

In this uncongenial place the simple storytelling script of *The Alcestiad* had to be blown up to near-pageantry proportions. There were not the words to cover the added action and the crowd scenes that filled the stage and trailed down the aisles under Tyrone Guthrie's exciting but overdramatic direction. Good or bad the *play* was nearly lost.

Even the title was changed to *A Life in the Sun*, which the management thought would have "more box-office appeal." Thornton refers to this in a letter from Scotland to our brother Amos in Cambridge, Massachusetts:

> That's *The Alcestiad*, but the entrepreneurs hate that for a title. . . . *A Life in the Sun* is a pretty cheery title for a play fraught with dire events, but it says that Alcestis's life is rooted in Apollo and there's a deal about his being the Sun, so there you are. . . .

There were compensations for Thornton. He was not one to despair, nor even fret long. Guthrie's extraordinary talents lighted up some passages, the rare Irene Worth headed a strong cast, and most of the public seated in those uncomfortable rows were gratifyingly responsive and definite in their approval, although the critics, as they do more often than not, veered from appreciative interest and understanding to omniscient disdain.

Most important of all, the author saw his work as a living whole in three-dimensional form. He learned what he had or had not accomplished to his own satisfaction. He also received balm for having felt betrayed by The Church of Scotland Assembly Hall when Tyrone Guthrie very magnanimously confided to him, "I did not serve your play well."

There was much interest among theatrical producers in this country and elsewhere in obtaining the rights for a New York production. My brother had his own ideas as to what changes he wished to make in the text. He talked with a number of directors and listened to their suggestions. He began working on revisions. This always was difficult for him; he was at his best living in the present and looking into the future. Too many people were giving him advice, crowding him. "I need a longer perspective," he told them. He withdrew the script from circulation, refusing acting rights to those who were willing to try it out as it stood.

When he was released from the unaccustomed pressure, fresh ideas began to come to him for both *The Alcestiad* and the Satyr play he wanted to go with it in the proper tradition of Greek dramaturgy. He was soon enthralled with *The Drunken Sisters*. It was one of those works that the writer—or composer in any medium—experiences occasionally. It "came" to him all at once on a single direct line, unfolding from beginning to end. Few changes had to be made in the original manuscript for its appearance in the *Atlantic Monthly* in 1957.

With *The Drunken Sisters* demanding to be heard and seen on a stage, it was not difficult for my brother to be persuaded to sign a contract for the two plays to be presented at the Schausspielhaus in Zürich, Switzerland. It was in this theater during the Second World War that *Our Town* and *The Skin of Our Teeth* had had their first European presentations; many of the most distinguished German and Austrian *regisseurs* and actors and actresses had sought refuge in Switzerland, and Thornton's works, fictional as well as dramatic, were well known to them and held in high regard.

Thornton worked with the translator, Herberth E. Herlitschka, a Viennese who had translated much of his earlier work into the German language. The revisions made at this time from the text performed at Edinburgh were not great, as he wanted to see the same play interpreted by another director and another cast. It was an exciting and stunning production in every way, the kind of evening in the theater that has the audience alert, arguing between the acts, clapping hard at the curtains, and leaving the theater full of life.

The Zürich opening was followed by full-scale productions in most of the state-endowed theaters in the large and small cities throughout Germany. It was presented also at the Burg Theater in Vienna. During this period, Thornton made further revisions and, responding to the great demand in Germany, permitted publication of a German edition, by Fischer Verlag, in 1960.

The play was discussed in the literary sections of newspapers and magazines and in scholarly journals and books. Käte Hamburger, in her volume on classical figures in modern literature, *From Sophocles to Sartre,** wrote: "Wilder's work is the most significant interpretation of the [Alcestis] theme in modern world literature."

Though Thornton did not continue to work on *The Alcestiad*

---

*New York: Ungar, 1969. Translation of *Von Sophokles zu Sartre, Griechische Dramenfiguren Antik und Modern*, Stuttgart, 1962.

as a play-script in English, he could not let it go. It seemed inevitable that when he started searching for a subject for an opera libretto for Louise Talma, whose musical compositions he admired greatly, the circle would be completed.

The opera, also entitled *The Alcestiad,* was six years in the making. It opened in the splendid, rebuilt opera house of Frankfurt, Germany, on March 2, 1962. It is opera on a grand scale requiring a large stage, a large orchestra, a large cast. The production, backed with a subsidy, was given all these elements, and Inge Borkh was a superb Alcestis. The final curtain came down to storybook, thunderous applause and cries of "bravo." There were over thirty curtain calls. Miss Talma, Thornton, everybody were called and re-called to take bows. The rejoicing was great at the dinner party after the performance. Yet the critics' reviews during the next few days and later in the weekly journals were very mixed. One veiled but definite complaint that came through in the most unsympathetic was that women should not write operas, another that the music was too modern.

For his part Thornton was completely satisfied with the score, and felt that any fault in the work came from his inexperience as a librettist. The opera has since been given in concert form, and arias from it have been sung in various recitals. Thornton never doubted that it was a work ahead of its time and would one day find full recognition.

Though my brother began writing early in life his list of accomplishments is not long: seven novels; some telling essays and introductions to books—his own and others—two volumes of short plays and four major long ones, counting *The Merchant of Yonkers* and *The Matchmaker* as one. In his work he was not afraid to repeat himself or to be influenced by the masters in the tradition of literature who had passed the torch from hand to hand.

Of his theater pieces he wrote in the preface to the collected *Three Plays:* *

> I am not one of the new dramatists we are looking for. I wish I were.
> I hope I have played a part in preparing the way for them. I am not
> an innovator but a rediscoverer of forgotten goods and I hope a
> remover of obtrusive bric-a-brac.

But he experimented with form. He dared to play with chronological time, historical time, and literary time, plucking events from history, people from pedestals and picture frames, and characters from hallowed printed pages. He gave voice to death, angels, pagan gods, and animals.

In the Foreword to his collection of "three-minute" plays for reading, *The Angel That Troubled the Waters,* ** my brother wrote of the problems of a young writer (he knew, for he had written some of these plays while he was still in his teens). He described moments of elation and discouragement, and the possibilities:

> How different the practice of writing would be if one did not permit
> oneself to be pretentious. Some hands have no choice: they would
> rather fail with an oratorio than succeed with a ballad.

Thornton always believed firmly that a wastebasket was a writer's best friend. Even so, his extant papers give evidence of some of his own failed oratorios, including the first two acts—the third was never written—of *The Emporium,* a play set in the largest, most alluring store in the world, where you can find everything you need or think you want, and *The Melting Pot,* an unfinished scenario for an epic film on the growth of our country told through the lives of generations of people. But although he did not himself take time from other projects to revise the English text of *The Alcestiad* to agree with what he had authorized

*New York: Harper & Brothers, 1957.
**New York: Coward-McCann, 1928.

for publication in German, and would doubtless have made further revisions, the play as printed is no failed oratorio. It is a work that reflects successfully some of his most abiding convictions about the verities of human experience.

Thornton Wilder's tapestry is finished. With the publication of *The Alcestiad* with *The Drunken Sisters* and the telling of its story, the final design comes clear, revealing all that he did with his portion of the alphabet, with his talents, with the years given to him and, most of all, with what he believed and tried to share. Now that the last length of Alcestis's huge ball of yarn has been unwound and the last stitch knotted there are no further mysteries on the subject to be guarded at Delphi.

—ISABEL WILDER

Martha's Vineyard
July 1977

Acknowledgments

This volume would not have been possible without the loyal sponsorship of Cass Canfield, whom Thornton Wilder trusted and admired as publisher and friend for almost fifty years; nor without the good judgment and uncounted hours spent preparing the text from German and English sources by Donald C. Gallup, Curator of the American Collection in the Beinecke Rare Book and Manuscript Library, Yale University, and Literary Executor of Thornton Wilder; nor without words of counsel and encouragement from our brother, the Reverend Amos Niven Wilder, Hollis Professor of Divinity, Emeritus, the Harvard Divinity School. Thanks in abundance is offered to all three and also to my Harper editor, Corona Machemer, whose patience and expertise recommend her as pilot for a stout or fragile craft on calm or stormy waters.

THE

ALCESTIAD

THE ALCESTIAD

APOLLO
DEATH
FIRST WATCHMAN
ALCESTIS
AGLAIA
TEIRESIAS
BOY
ADMETUS
FIRST HERDSMAN
SECOND HERDSMAN
THIRD HERDSMAN
FOURTH HERDSMAN
RHODOPE
HERCULES
SECOND WATCHMAN
EPIMENES
CHERIANDER
AGIS
FIRST GUARD
SECOND GUARD
THIRD GUARD
FOURTH GUARD
SERVANTS
PEOPLE OF THESSALY

THE DRUNKEN SISTERS

APOLLO
CLOTHO
LACHESIS } THE THREE FATES
ATROPOS

The Alcestiad was first performed with the title *A Life in the Sun* at The Church of Scotland Assembly Hall, The Mound, Edinburgh, on August 22, 1955. It was produced by the Edinburgh Festival Society in association with Tennent Productions Limited and was directed by Tyrone Guthrie, with décor by Tanya Moiseiwitsch. The cast* was as follows:

APOLLO	MICHAEL DAVID
DEATH	JOHN KIDD
FIRST WATCHMAN	LAURENCE HARDY
ALCESTIS	IRENE WORTH
AGLAIA	MADELEINE CHRISTIE
TEIRESIAS	GEOFFREY DUNN
BOY	DAVID GLOAG
ADMETUS	ROBERT HARDY
FIRST HERDSMAN	PHILIP GUARD
SECOND HERDSMAN	JOHN SCHOLAN
THIRD HERDSMAN	PETER FOX
FOURTH HERDSMAN	PETER DUGUID
HERCULES	RUPERT DAVIES
SECOND WATCHMAN	PETER BAYLISS
EPIMENES	ALEXANDER DAVION
CHERIANDER	MICHAEL BATES
AGIS	ROBERT SPEAIGHT
FIRST GUARD	MICHAEL ALLINSON
SECOND GUARD	TIMOTHY FINDLEY
THIRD GUARD	JOHN GREIG
FOURTH GUARD	DAVID SAXBY
SERVANTS	JENNIFER WRIGHT, MARY WYLIE
PEOPLE OF THESSALY	WILLIAM ROBERTSON, JOHN MACDONALD, WILLIAM LYON BROWN, JOYCE ALLAN, BETTY THORBURN, JOYCE C. KERR, ANN TIRARD, HELENA GLOAG, ANN GIBSON, PETER SMALLWOOD, PAT MAGEE

*The name of the actress playing RHODOPE was inadvertently omitted from the program.

ACT I

No curtain, except at the end of Act III and after *The Drunken Sisters*. All three acts of *The Alcestiad* take place in the rear court of the palace of ADMETUS, King of Thessaly, many centuries before the Great Age of Greece. Each act begins at dawn and ends at sunset of the same day.

The palace is a low, squat house of roughly dressed stone, with a flat roof. There is a suggestion of a portico, however, supported by sections of the trunks of great trees. The palace doors are of wood and a gilded ox skull is affixed to each of them. Before these doors is a platform with low steps leading down to the soil floor of the courtyard.

The front of the palace fills the left three-quarters of the back of the stage. The rest of the stage is enclosed by clay-brick walls. In the wall to the right is a large wooden gate leading to the road outside and to the city of Pherai. The wall on the left is less high; a small door in it leads to the servants' quarters.

From the front center of the stage a path leads down (descending to the right) to what in a conventional theater would be the orchestra pit. At the bottom of this path is a "grotto"—a spring with practical flowing water; a bronze door to the Underworld, overhung by vines, but large enough for actors to pass through. Here is also (not seen, only assumed) the snake PYTHO.

First streaks of dawn.

Gradually a light rises to brilliancy, revealing APOLLO *standing on the roof of the palace. He wears a costume of gold with a long dark-blue*

5

mantle over his right shoulder. A blue light begins to glow from the entrance to Hell, down by the spring. DEATH—*in a garment of large black patches, in which he looks like a bat or a beetle—comes waddling up the path and sniffs at the gate left and at the palace gate.*
Throughout the scene APOLLO *gazes off toward the rising sun—cool, measured, and with a faint smile on His lips.*

APOLLO:

> *Like a "Good morning."*

Death!

DEATH:

Aaah! You are here! The palace of Admetus has an honored guest! We are to have a wedding here today. What a guest! Or have you come to steal the bride away, illustrious Apollo?

APOLLO:

Death, you live in the dark.

DEATH:

I do, I do. Have you come, Lord Apollo, to show us some great sign, some wonder today?

> *The* NIGHT WATCHMAN, *sounding his rattle and carrying a waxed parchment lantern, comes around the palace, up center.*

WATCHMAN:

> *Singsong.*

The watch before dawn, and all is well in the palace of Admetus the Hospitable, King of Thessaly, rich in horses.

> *Starting to go off left.*

Dawn. The day of the wedding—of the greatest of all weddings.

> *Exit left into the servants' quarters.*

6

DEATH:

I was asking, Lord Apollo, if you had come to show us some great wonder.

Pause.

Yes? No? "Yes," I hope. When the gods come near to men, sooner or later someone is killed. Am I to welcome some admired guest in my kingdom today? Am I to have King Admetus or the Princess Alcestis?

APOLLO:

No.

DEATH:

I shall watch and hope.

He waddles to the center.

In which of your powers and capacities are you here today, may I ask? As healer?

Pause.

As bringer of light and life?

Pause.

As singer?

APOLLO:

Still gazing off, casually.

They are all one and the same. I have come to set a song in motion —a story—

DEATH:

A story!

APOLLO:

A story that will be told many times . . .

DEATH:

Ah! A lesson! Will there be a lesson in it for me?

APOLLO:

Yes.

DEATH:

Beating with his flippers on the ground.

No!

APOLLO:

Yes. You are to learn something.

DEATH:

Scuttling about in rage.

No! There is no lesson you can teach me. I am here forever, and I do not change. It's you Gods of the Upper Air that need lessons. And I'll read you a lesson right now.

Shrilly.

Leave these human beings alone. Stay up on Mount Olympus, where you belong, and enjoy yourselves. I've watched this foolishness coming over you for a long time. You made these creatures and then you became infatuated with them. You've thrown the whole world into confusion and it's getting worse every day. All you do is to torment them—who knows better than I?

He waddles back to the top of the path, shaking himself furiously.

They will never understand your language. The more you try to say something, the more you drive them distraught.

APOLLO:

They have begun to understand me. At first they were like the beasts—more savage, more fearful. Like beasts in a cage, themselves the cage to themselves. Then two things broke on their minds and they lifted their heads: my father's thunder, which raised their fears to awe; and my sunlight, for which they gave thanks. In thanks they discovered speech, and I gave them song.

These were signs and they knew them. First one, then another, knew that I prompted their hearts and was speaking.

DEATH:

Yes, they're not like they used to be: "Apollo *loves* Thessaly. Apollo *loves* the house of Pherai." Go back to Olympus, where you belong. All this loving . . . It's hard to tell which is the unhappier—you or these wretched creatures. When you try to come into their lives you're like a giant in a small room: with every movement you break something. And whom are you tormenting today? The King? Or his bride?

APOLLO:

You.

DEATH:

Me? Me? So you've decided to love me, too? No, thank you!
> *He flaps all his flippers, scrambles down the path, then scrambles up again; shrilly.*

You can't trouble me, and you can't give me any lessons. I and my Kingdom were made to last forever. How could you possibly trouble me?

APOLLO:

You live in the dark and you cannot see that all things change.

DEATH:

> *Screaming.*

Change! There'll be no change.
> *He looks around in apprehension.*

It's getting light. And this story you're starting today is about a change? A change for *me*?

APOLLO:

For you and for me.

9

DEATH:

> *Disappearing into his cave, with one last sneering scream.*

For *you!*

> *The light on* APOLLO *fades and he disappears.*
> *The* WATCHMAN *returns on his rounds. He shakes his rattle,*
> *then blows out the lamp.*

WATCHMAN:

Dawn. Dawn. And all is well in the palace of Admetus the Hospitable, King of Thessaly, rich in horses.

> *Descends toward audience.*

It is the day of the wedding, the greatest of all weddings, and all is *not* well. Why can't she sleep—the princess, the bride, our future queen? Eight, ten times during the night, I've found her here—wandering about, looking at the sky. Sometimes she goes out into the road, as though she were waiting for a messenger. She stands here and raises her arms—whispers: "Apollo! A sign! One sign!" Sign of what? That she is right to marry King Admetus? Eh! Where will she find clearer signs than those written on his face? Oh, I have lived a long time. I know that a bride can be filled with fears on the night before her wedding. But to be afraid of our Admetus who has won her hand in such a wonderful way that all Greece is amazed. Oh, my friends, take an old watchman's advice. Don't meditate upon the issues of life at three in the morning. At that hour no warmth reaches your heart and mind. At that hour—huuu—you see your house in flames and your children stretched out dead at your feet. Wait until the sun rises. The facts are the same—the facts of a human life are the same—but the sunlight gives them a meaning. Take the advice of a night watchman. Now I want a drink of water.

> *He descends to the spring and greets the snake* PYTHO.

Good day to you, Pytho, old friend. It will be a great day for you, too. You shall have a part in the marriage banquet—a great sheep, or half an ox. Now come! Leave my hands free to make the offering.

> *He lets the water slip through his cupped hands. And mumbles the ritual: "You sources of life—earth, air, fire, and water . . ." Then he scoops once more and drinks. He addresses the audience.*

Look, friends. Do you see this cave under the vines? This is one of the five entrances into Hell, and our good Pytho is here to guard it. No man has ever entered it, and no man has ever come out of it. That's what it is—merely one of the ten thousand things we do not understand.

> *He drinks again. Shriek of a slain animal.*

Well, the great day has begun. They are slaughtering the animals for the feast. The cooks are building great fires. The meadows are filled with the tents of kings and of chiefs who have come to celebrate the wedding of King Admetus, and of the Princess Alcestis, daughter of Pelias, King of Iolcos.

> *He starts up the path.* ALCESTIS, *in white, glides out of the palace doors. Animal cries.*

Hsst! There she is again!

> *He hides on the path below the level of the stage.* ALCESTIS *comes to the center of the stage, raises her arms, and whispers:*

ALCESTIS:

Apollo! A sign! One sign!

> *She goes out the gate, right, leading to the road.*

WATCHMAN:

> *Softly to the audience, mimicking her.*

Apollo! One sign!

> *Animal cries.* AGLAIA, *the old nurse, comes out quickly from the palace. She looks about, sees the* WATCHMAN.

11

AGLAIA:

> *Whispers:*

Where is the princess?

> *He points.*

All night—this restlessness, this unhappiness! "Apollo! One sign!"

WATCHMAN:

"Apollo! One sign!"

> ALCESTIS *comes in from the gate, in nervous decisiveness.*

ALCESTIS:

Watchman!

WATCHMAN:

Yes, Princess?

ALCESTIS:

Find my drivers. Tell them to harness the horses for a journey. Aglaia, call together my maids; tell them to get everything ready.

AGLAIA:

A journey, Princess—on your wedding day, a journey?

ALCESTIS:

> *Who has swept by her; from the palace steps.*

Aglaia, I have no choice in this. I must go. Forgive me. No, hate me; despise me—but finally forget me.

AGLAIA:

Princess, the shame—and the insult to King Admetus.

ALCESTIS:

I know all that, Aglaia. Aglaia, when I have gone, tell the King —tell Admetus—that I take all the shame; that I do not ask him to forgive me, but to despise me and forget me.

AGLAIA:

Princess, I am an old woman. I am no ordinary slave in this house. I nursed the child Admetus and his father before him.
To the WATCHMAN.
Watchman, leave us alone.
Exit WATCHMAN.
You do not know King Admetus. In all Greece and the Islands you would not find a better husband.

ALCESTIS:
I know this.

AGLAIA:

You will find men who are more warlike, more adventurous, stronger perhaps—but not one more just, more . . . more beloved.

ALCESTIS:

All this I know, Aglaia. I, too, love Admetus. Because of that I am doubly unhappy. But there is One I love more.

AGLAIA:

Another? Another man? Above Admetus? Then go, Princess, and go quickly. We have been mistaken in you. You have no business here. If you have no eyes; if you have no mind; if you cannot see—
Harshly.
Watchman! Watchman! Everything will be ready for your journey, Princess. But go quickly.

ALCESTIS:

No, Aglaia, not another man. The thing that I love more than Admetus is . . . is a God. Is Apollo.

AGLAIA:
Apollo?

ALCESTIS:

Yes. Since a young girl I have had only one wish—to be His priestess at Delphi.

> *She despairs of expressing herself. Then suddenly cries, with passion:*

I wish to live in the real. With one life to live, one life to give—not these lives we see about us: fever and pride and . . . and possessionship—but in the real; at Delphi, where the truth is.

AGLAIA:

But the God has not called you?

> *Pause.*

The God has not sent for you?

ALCESTIS:

> *Low; in shame.*

No.

AGLAIA:

And this real—it is not real enough to be the wife of Admetus, the mother of his children, and the Queen of Thessaly?

ALCESTIS:

Any woman can be wife and mother; and hundreds have been queens. My husband. My children. To center your life upon these five or six, to be bound and shut in with everything that concerns them . . . each day filled—so filled—with the thousand occupations that help or comfort them, that finally one sinks into the grave loved and honored, but as ignorant as the day one was born—

AGLAIA:

Ignorant?

ALCESTIS:

Knowing as little of why we live and why we die—of why the hundred thousand live and die—as the day we were born.

AGLAIA:

> *Dryly.*

And that you think you can learn at Delphi? But the God has not called you.

ALCESTIS:

> *In shame.*

I sent offerings . . . messages . . . offerings . . .

> *Pause.*

I was my father's favorite daughter. He wished me never to marry, but to remain with him until his death. But suitors came to seek my hand from all Greece. He imposed upon them an impossible task. He required of them that they yoke together a lion and a boar and drive them thrice about the walls of our city of Iolcos. They came from all Greece: Jason came, and Nestor; Hercules, son of Zeus, came; and Atreus. And all failed. Month after month the new suitors failed and barely escaped with their lives. My father and I sat at the city gates and my father laughed. And I smiled—not because I wished to live with my father, but because I wished for only this one thing: to live and die as a priestess of Apollo at Delphi.

AGLAIA:

And then Admetus came. And he drove the lion and the boar— like mild oxen he drove them about the city; and won your hand, Princess.

ALCESTIS:

But I loved Apollo more.

15

AGLAIA:

Yes. But it was Apollo who made this marriage.

ALCESTIS:

We cannot know that.

AGLAIA:

The sign you are asking for, Princess, is before you—the clearest of signs.

> *Drastically.*

You have not been called to Delphi: you cannot read the simplest words of the God.

> ALCESTIS *shields her face.*

Now listen to what I am telling you: were you not amazed that Admetus was able to yoke together the lion and the boar? Where Atreus failed, and Hercules, son of Zeus? I will tell you how he did it: in a dream, the God Apollo taught him how to yoke together a lion and a boar.

> ALCESTIS *takes two steps backward.*

First, he saw and loved you. Before he returned to Iolcos that second time—after his first failure—he fell ill. Love and despair brought him to the point of death—and I nursed him. Three nights he lay at the point of death. And the third night, I was sitting beside him—his agony and his delirium—and I heard, I *saw*, that in a dream Apollo was teaching him to yoke together a lion and a boar.

> ALCESTIS *gazes at her.*

This is true. I swear it is true.

ALCESTIS:

True, yes—but we have heard enough of these deliriums and dreams, fevers and visions. Aglaia, it is time we asked for certainties. The clear open presence of the God—that is at Delphi.

AGLAIA:

Clear? Open? Even at Delphi the sibyl is delirious; she raves; she is beside herself. Who ever heard of them speaking clearly?

ALCESTIS:

Turning with irresolute step toward the palace, in despair.
I am alone, alone. . . .

AGLAIA:

Firmly but affectionately.
Now listen to me, Princess. Go to your room and sleep.
Looking upward.
It is two hours to noon. If, after a little rest, you are still of the same mind, you can go on any journey you want, and no one will try to stop you.
Holding ALCESTIS's elbow, she guides her to the palace doors, prattling in maternal fashion.
You want the gods to speak to us clearly and openly, Princess? What can you be thinking they are, Princess? I hope you don't think of them as men!
Both exit into the palace. For a moment the stage is empty. A sound of voices at the gate rises almost to clamor. Pounding and knocking at right. The WATCHMAN comes around the palace up center.

WATCHMAN:

Well, now, what's that? What's all this noise?
Opens the gate and talks through it, ajar.
The wedding guests enter at the gate in front of the palace. This is the rear gate. What? Don't everybody talk at once! What? Very well, very well. Let the old man in.
Enter TEIRESIAS, blind, unbelievably old, irascible, truculent, domineering, and very near to senile incoherence. One hand is on the shoulder of a BOY who guides him; the other ceaselessly

17

brandishes a great stick. TOWNSPEOPLE *follow him into the court; and some* SERVANTS *come into the court both from the palace doors and from around the palace.*

TEIRESIAS:

> *Surprisingly loud and strong.*

Is this the palace of Minos, King of Crete?

> *Laughter; the* BOY *starts pulling his sleeve and whispering into his ear.*

I mean, is this the palace of Oedipus, King of Thebes?

> *Striking the* BOY *with his stick.*

Stop pulling at me! I know what I'm saying.

> *Warding off those pressing about him.*

Bees, wasps, and hornets!

WATCHMAN:

No, old man. This is the palace of Admetus, King of Thessaly.

TEIRESIAS:

> *Repeating his words.*

King of Thessaly. Well, that's what I said. That's what I meant. Call Admetus, King of Thessaly. I have a message for him.

WATCHMAN:

Old man, the King is to be married today. He is busy with his guests. You sit here in the sun now; we shall wash your feet. The King will come and hear you later.

TEIRESIAS:

> *Threatening with his stick.*

Marrying . . . washing. What have I got to do with marrying and washing? I'll not wait a minute.

> *Stamping.*

Call King What's-his-name.

> *Enter* AGLAIA *from the palace.*

18

AGLAIA:

Who are you, old man? I shall tell the King—

TEIRESIAS:

Tell the King that I am Delphi, priest of Teiresias—Apollo, priest of Delphi. . . . Boy, what is this I'm saying?

> BOY *whispers.*

Tell the King I am Teiresias, priest of Apollo. That I come from Delphi with a message and that I am in a hurry to go back there.

AGLAIA:

You are Teiresias? Teiresias!

WATCHMAN and BYSTANDERS:

Teiresias!

TEIRESIAS:

> *Beating with his stick on the ground.*

Call the King! Plague and pestilence! Call King What's-his-name.

AGLAIA:

Coming, great Teiresias.

> *She is hurrying to the palace door as it opens and* ADMETUS *comes out. More* SERVANTS *gather.*

ADMETUS:

What is it? Who is this, Aglaia?

AGLAIA:

> *Confidentially.*

It is Teiresias, come from Delphi.

ADMETUS:

Teiresias!

19

AGLAIA:

>*Points to her forehead.*

As old as the mountains, King Admetus.

ADMETUS:

Welcome, welcome, noble Teiresias, my father's old friend. Welcome to Pherai. I am Admetus, King of Thessaly.

TEIRESIAS:

>*Waving his stick.*

Back. Stand back. All this crowding and pushing . . . Have you ears, fellow?

ADMETUS:

Yes, Teiresias.

TEIRESIAS:

Then pull the wax out of them and listen to what the God says.

ADMETUS:

They are open, Teiresias.

TEIRESIAS:

Atreus, King of Mycenae, hear what the God says—

ADMETUS:

Atreus? Noble Teiresias, I am Admetus, King of—

TEIRESIAS:

Admetus? All right—Admetus, then. Hold your tongue and let me get my message out. I bring a message to you from Apollo's temple at Delphi. An honor, a great honor has come to Thessaly. Boy, is this Thessaly?

>*He puts hands on the* BOY's *head; the* BOY *nods.*

A great honor and a great peril has come to Thessaly.

ADMETUS:

A peril, Teiresias?

TEIRESIAS:

An honor and a peril. A peril is an honor, fool. No—an honor is a peril. Don't you know the first things up here in Thessaly?

ADMETUS:

One moment, Teiresias. A message to me is also a message to my future queen. Aglaia, call the princess.
>AGLAIA *hurries into the palace.*
Today I am to be married to Alcestis, daughter of King Pelias of Iolcos. No guest is more to be honored than Teiresias. Rest first, Teiresias. . . .

TEIRESIAS:

There are ten thousand weddings. Let this queen make haste. Hear me, Minos, King of Crete. . . . Boy, what is his name?
>BOY *whispers.*
Well, what does it matter? Is this queen here?
>*Enter from the palace* ALCESTIS, *breathless with wonder.*

ADMETUS:

She is here.

ALCESTIS:

Noble Teiresias . . . great Teiresias! My father's old friend. I am Alcestis, daughter of King Pelias of Iolcos.

TEIRESIAS:

>*Waving his stick testily at those pressing around him.*
Back! Keep back! Geese and ducks and quacklings. Silence and hold your tongues. Zeus, father of gods and men, has commanded . . . has commanded . . . Boy, what has he commanded?
>BOY *whispers.* TEIRESIAS *strikes him.*

21

Well, you don't have to run on. . . . Has commanded that Apollo, my master—that Apollo come down from Olympus; and that he live on earth for one year, solstice to solstice . . . live as a man among men. I have given my message. Boy, lead me to the road.

He turns to go.

ALCESTIS:

While the BOY *whispers into* TEIRESIAS'S *ear.*
Apollo is to live on the earth?

TEIRESIAS:

To the BOY.
Yes, yes. Don't deafen me. And Apollo, my master, has chosen to live here—

He strikes the ground with his stick.
here as a servant of Admetus, King of Thessaly.

ADMETUS:

Here? Here, noble Teiresias?

Goes quickly to him.
One moment more, Teiresias. How do I understand this? You do not mean, divine Teiresias, that Apollo will be here, with us, as a servant, every day? With us, each day?

As all watch him breathlessly, TEIRESIAS, *hand to brow, seems to fall into a deep sleep. Suddenly he awakes and says:*

TEIRESIAS:

Outside the gate are four herdsmen. They are to be your servants for a year. Assign them their duties. One of them is Apollo.

ADMETUS:

Repeating.
One of them is Apollo?

TEIRESIAS:

Four herdsmen. One of them is Apollo. Do not try to know which one is the God. I do not know. You will never know. And ask me no more questions, for I have no more answers. Boy, call the herdsmen.

The BOY *goes out. Silence.*

ADMETUS:

Teiresias, should we not . . . fall on our knees, on our faces?

TEIRESIAS:

You do not listen to what's said to you. Apollo is here, *as a man.* As a man. As a common herdsman or shepherd. . . . Do as I do!

The BOY *returns and presses close to* TEIRESIAS. *Enter the* FOUR HERDSMEN. *They are dusty, dirty, unshaven common oafs. They are deeply abashed by the great folk before them, touch their forelocks obsequiously, shuffle into a line against the wall, and don't know what to do with their eyes. Two have great wine-skins; all have big sticks.* TEIRESIAS *speaks gruffly to them.*

TEIRESIAS:

Come, don't be slow about it. Make your bow to your new master. Anyone can see you've been drinking. A nice way to begin your service.

Waving his stick.

If I had eyes to see, I'd beat you. Forward; pick up your feet. Boy, are they all four here? Well, has the King lost his voice?

ADMETUS:

Pulling himself together.

You are welcome to Thessaly. You are welcome to the wedding feast, for I am to be married today. Tomorrow I shall assign you your herds and flocks. You have made a long journey. You are welcome to Thessaly. . . . Teiresias, you, too, have made a long journey. Will you not bathe and rest?

TEIRESIAS:

I have a longer journey to go. My message has been delivered. Boy, lead me out the gate.

ALCESTIS:

> *Coming to a few steps before him; in a low voice.*
Divine Teiresias? Have you no message for Alcestis?

TEIRESIAS:

Who's this woman?

ALCESTIS:

I am Alcestis, daughter of King Pelias of Iolcos. I sent many messages and offerings to Delphi and—

TEIRESIAS:

Messages and offerings. There are mountains of them. Boy, lead me to the road.

> *But the* BOY *keeps pulling at his sleeve and shoulder and trying to whisper to him.*

Oh, yes, I had a message for some girl or woman—for Jocasta, or Alcestis, or Dejaneira, or I care not whom, but I have forgotten it. Boy, stop dragging at me!

> *He strikes the* BOY *with his stick.*

Worthless! Impudent!

> *The* BOY *falls.* TEIRESIAS *continues to beat him.*

BOY:

> *Screaming.*
Teiresias! Help! Help! King Admetus!

ADMETUS:
Surely, great Teiresias, the boy has not—

ALCESTIS:
It was a small fault, Teiresias. I beg you spare the boy. He will learn.

TEIRESIAS:
> *Suddenly stopping and peering at* ALCESTIS.

Whatever your name is: Jocasta, Leda, Hermione—

ALCESTIS:
Alcestis.

TEIRESIAS:
I had a message for some girl, but I have forgotten it. Or else I've delivered it already. That's it: I've delivered it. By thunder and lightning, by the holy tripod—what use is Delphi if men and women cannot learn to listen?

> TEIRESIAS *is following the* BOY *out of the gate, when* ADMETUS *takes some steps forward.*

ADMETUS:
You said . . . you said there was peril, Teiresias?

TEIRESIAS:
> *Half out of the gate.*

Of course there's peril, imbecile. When they
> *Brusque gesture upward.*

draw near it is always peril.

ADMETUS:
But my father said that Apollo has always loved Thessaly. . . .

TEIRESIAS:
Yes—love, love, love. Let them keep their love to themselves. Look at me: five—six hundred years old and pretty well loved by

25

the gods and I am not allowed to die. If the gods didn't love men, we'd all be happy; and the other way round is true, too: if we men didn't love the gods, we'd all be happy.

Exit, with the BOY.

A bewildered pause.

ADMETUS *collects himself and says in a more matter-of-fact, authoritative tone to the* FOUR HERDSMEN:

ADMETUS:

Again, you are welcome to Thessaly and to Pherai.

To the WATCHMAN.

See that they are well provided for.

Again to the HERDSMEN.

I am happy that you are to be guests at my wedding today.

ADMETUS *and all on the stage watch in confused awe as the* WATCHMAN *guides them down the path to the spring. They pass* ADMETUS *with servile timidity; by the spring they stretch out, pass the wineskin from one to another; one promptly falls asleep.* ADMETUS *has not looked at* ALCESTIS. *Partly to her and partly to himself, he says reflectively:*

I do not know what to think of these things. . . . I am a mere herdsman myself. Alcestis, there is great need of you in Pherai.

He stretches his hand out behind him. She, frozen in thought, does not take it.

I must return to my guests.

With a last echo of his awe.

I do not know what to think of these things.

Then with a smile.

Alcestis, there is an old custom here in Thessaly that a bridegroom should not see the face of his bride until the evening of his wedding day. This has been said for many hundreds of years. Is there also such a custom at Iolcos?

ALCESTIS:

Low.
Yes, Admetus.

ADMETUS:

Passing her with youthful vigor, his hand shielding his face.
Hereafter—by the God's gift—I may look upon your face until
I die.

*At the door of the palace, he is arrested by a thought. Still
shielding his face, he comes in slow deliberation to the point of
the stage, overhanging the* HERDSMEN *by the spring. After
taking a deep breath of resolution, he says with unemphatic
directness:*
Apollo, friend of my father and my ancestors and my land, I am
a simple man, devout. I am not learned in piety. If, in ignorance,
I blunder and fall short, may He who has been the friend of my
house and my people forgive me. You have come on a day when
I am the happiest of all men. Continue your favor to me and to
my descendants. . . .

Slight pause.
I am not skilled in speech. You can read all minds. Read what is
in mine, or rather . . . yourself plant in my mind those wishes
which only you can fulfill.

He turns and goes quickly into the palace.

ALCESTIS:

Who has not ceased to keep her eyes on the HERDSMEN, *half in
longing and half in doubt and repulsion—though they are now
hidden from where she is standing, murmuring.*
Is Apollo there?

AGLAIA:

Princess!

27

ALCESTIS:

One of those? And could that old man have been Teiresias of Delphi—that broken, crazy old man?

AGLAIA:

Really shocked; firmly.
Do not doubt these things, Princess.

ALCESTIS:

After taking a few steps toward them; in sudden resolve.
Leave me alone with them.

> AGLAIA *makes a gesture to the* WATCHMAN *and both go out. During the following speech, though one* HERDSMAN *is asleep and snoring, the others are embarrassed by her presence. The wineskin is being passed around; they scarcely dare to raise their eyes to her.*

Are you here? I have spoken to you a thousand times—to the sky and the stars and the sun. And I have sent messages to Delphi. Are you now, truly, within the hearing of my voice?

> *Silence, broken by a snore and a grunt.*

Some say that you do not exist. Some say that the gods are far away; they are feasting on Olympus, or are asleep, or drunk. I have offered you my life. You know that I have wished to live only for you: to learn—to be taught by you—the meaning of our life.

> *No answer.*

Are we human beings to be left without any sign, any word? Are we abandoned?

> *She waits another second above the embarrassed silence of the* HERDSMEN, *then turns toward the palace, and says to herself, bitterly:*

Then we must find our way by ourselves . . . and life is a meaningless grasping at this and that; it is a passionate nonsense. . . .

The First Herdsman—*the dirtiest, most insignificant of the four—rises. He touches his cap in humble embarrassment and says:*

HERDSMAN:

Princess, did that old man say that there was a god among us? Did I hear him say that? The God Apollo? Then, lady, I am as surprised as you are. Lady, for thirty days we four have walked all across Greece. We have drunk from the same wineskin; we have put our hands in the same dish; we have slept by the same fire. If there had been a god among us, would I not have known it?

> Alcestis, *in hope and revulsion, has taken several steps toward him.*

By all I value, lady, I swear we are just ordinary herdsmen. Ignorant herdsmen. But . . . but one thing I will say, lady: we are not quite ordinary herdsmen. Why, that fellow there—the one that's snoring: there's no illness he cannot cure. Snakebite or a broken back. Yet I know that he is not a god, Princess. And that fellow beside him, that one!

> *He goes forward and kicks the* Herdsman.

Can't you stop drinking while the princess is looking at you? He never loses his way. In the darkest night he knows his north from his south and his east from his west. Oh, it's wonderful. Yet I know well that he's not the god of the sun.

> *Adding under his breath:*

Besides, his habits are filthy, are filthy.

ALCESTIS:

> *Barely breathing it.*

And that one?

HERDSMAN:

That man? He's our singer.

29

ALCESTIS:
Ah!

HERDSMAN:
Believe me, when he plays the lyre and sings—oh, Princess! It is true that at times I have said to myself, "Surely this is a god." He can fill us to the brim with joy or sadness when we have no reason at all to be joyful or sad. He can make the memory of love more sweet than love itself. But, Princess, he is no god.

> *As though she had contradicted him; with sudden argumentative energy.*

How can he be a god when he's in misery all the time and drinking himself to death? Killing himself, you might say, before our own eyes. The gods don't hate themselves, Princess.

ALCESTIS:
And you?

HERDSMAN:
I? *I*, Apollo? Not only am I not Apollo, but I'm not ready to believe that Apollo is here.

ALCESTIS:
Teiresias . . . Teiresias said . . .

HERDSMAN:
Was that Teiresias—that half-witted, crumbling old man? Can they find no better messenger than that? Can't they say what they have to say in any clearer way than this?

> *Again* ALCESTIS *turns toward the palace; then turns toward the* HERDSMAN *and says, as though talking to herself:*

ALCESTIS:
Then we are indeed miserable. Not only because we have no aid, but because we are cheated with the hope that we might have aid. . . .

HERDSMAN:
>*Taking more steps onto the stage.*

But if they did exist, these gods, how would they speak to us? In what language would they talk to us? Compared to them, we are diseased and dying and deaf and blind and as busy as clowns. Why, there are some who even say that they love us. Could you understand that? What kind of love is that, Princess, when there is so great a gulf between the lovers?

>*He starts to return to his place in the path.*

That would be an unhappy love, no doubt about that.

ALCESTIS:
>*Earnestly and sharply.*

No, not unhappy!

HERDSMAN:
>*With equal spirit.*

Yes. For if they showed themselves to us in their glory, it would kill us.

>*Pause.*

I did have an idea this morning: maybe there is another way— a way to bridge that gulf, I mean. Maybe they can find a way to bring those they love up—up nearer to them. If Teiresias is right, Apollo is here in Thessaly. Now, maybe that foolish old man got his message wrong. Maybe he was supposed to say that Apollo is here divided up among many people—us four herdsmen and others! Take Admetus, for example. I've only seen him for a few hours. I must confess, Princess, at first I was very disappointed in Admetus. There's nothing very extraordinary about him. Did you ever see Hercules, Princess?

ALCESTIS:
>*Nods her head slightly.*

Yes.

HERDSMAN:

> *Suddenly recollecting.*

Ah, yes. He sought your hand. There's a man! Hercules, son of Zeus and Alcmene. And you can see it at once. I've seen a dozen better men than Admetus. But . . . slowly I began to see that King Admetus has something that all those other heroes haven't got. . . . The world changes; it changes slowly. What good would this world be, Princess, unless new kinds of men came into it—and new kinds of women?

> *Enter* ADMETUS, *wearing on his right shoulder a light-blue cloak like Apollo's. He stands watching from the top step.*

And wouldn't that be, maybe, the way those unhappy lovers

> *He points upward.*

would try to throw a bridge across the gulf I was talking about?

> *He becomes aware of* ADMETUS. *Obsequiously bowing his head, and pulling his forelock, murmuring.*

We wish you all happiness . . . many years.

> *He goes back to his place.*
> *The sun is setting. The sky behind the palace roof is filled with color.*

ADMETUS:

> *With set face.*

Aglaia has told me of your wish to leave, Princess Alcestis. You are, of course, free to go. There are no constraints here. There are no slaves in Thessaly, Princess—not even its queen. I have just given orders that your drivers and your maids be prepared for the journey.

> *He takes one step down.*

Before you leave, I wish to say one thing. I do not say this in order to win your pity, nor to dissuade you from what you have planned to do. I say this because you and I are not children; and we should not conceal from one another what is in our hearts.

Slight pause.

It is still a great wonder to me that I was able to yoke the lion and the boar. But I am in no doubt as to *why* I was able to do it: I loved you. I shall never see you again. I shall never marry. And I shall never be the same. From now on I shall know that there is something wrong and false in this world into which we have been born. I am an ordinary man, but the love that filled me is not an ordinary love. When such love is not met by a love in return, then life is itself a deception. And it is best that men live at random, as best they may. For justice . . . and honor . . . and love are just things we invent for a short time, as suits the moment. May you have a good journey, Princess Alcestis.

> ALCESTIS *has been standing with raised head but lowered eyes. She now puts out her hand.*

ALCESTIS:

Admetus.

> *Slight pause.*

Admetus, ask me again to marry you.

> *He takes one quick step toward her; she again puts out her hand quickly to stop him.*

Ask me to love all the things that you love . . . and to be the queen of your Thessaly. Ask me in pain to bear you children. To walk beside you at the great festivals. To comfort you when you are despairing. To make sure that when you return from a journey the water for your bath will be hot, and that your house, Admetus, will be as well ordered as your mind. To live for you and for your children and for your people—to live for you as though every moment I were ready to die for you . . .

ADMETUS:

> *Joyously and loudly.*

No—no Alcestis! It is I . . .

He takes her outstretched hand. They do not embrace.
Alcestis, will you be the wife of Admetus, King of Thessaly?

ALCESTIS:
With my whole self, Admetus . . .
They go into the palace.

ACT II

The same scene, twelve years later.
Again first dawn. The same WATCHMAN *comes around the palace.*
He does not shake his rattle. He speaks softly, slowly, and dejectedly.

WATCHMAN:
The watch before dawn . . . the palace of Admetus the Hospitable, King of Thessaly, rich in horses.
He stands a moment, his eyes on the ground; then to the audience.
And all is as bad as it possibly could be . . . as it possibly could be.
He goes to the gate, which is ajar, and talks to a whispering crowd outside.
No, my friends. There is no news. The King is still alive; he has lived through another night. The Queen is sitting by his bed. She is holding his hand. . . . No news. No change. . . . Take that dog away; we must have no barking. Yes, the King drank some ox blood mixed with wine.
He returns to the center of the stage and addresses the audience.
Our King is at the point of death, there is no doubt about it. You remember those herdsmen, twelve years ago, that Teiresias brought here, saying that one of them was Apollo—and that Apollo would live here as a servant for a year? You remember all that?
Well, at the end of the year did they go away? No; all four of them

are still here. Was Apollo in one of them? Nobody knows. Don't try to think about it; you'll lose your senses if you try to understand things like that. But, friends, that first year was a wonderful year. I cannot explain this to you: it was no more or less prosperous than other years. To a visitor, to a passer-by, everything would have appeared the same. But to us who were living it, everything was different. The facts of our human life never change; it is our way of seeing them that changes. Apollo was certainly here.

Pause.

What? How did King Admetus come by his illness? Well, as I say, those four herdsmen stayed on. They were good fellows and good workers—though they talked south-country Greek. But two of them—eh!—drank their wine without water. And one evening at sunset time those two were sitting drinking—there, right there! —and a quarrel arose between them. There was shouting and chasing about, and King Admetus came out to put a stop to it. Then—oh, my friends—one of the herdsmen whipped out his knife and stabbed King Admetus by mistake, stabbed him from here

Points to his throat.

right down his side to the waist. You could put your hand in it. That was weeks ago. The wound didn't heal. It got angry and boiled and watered and boiled and watered, and now the King must surely die. No one's wanted to punish the herdsman whose body held Apollo—you see? And the crime may have been Apollo's will—try to think that through! And that herdsman's outside the gate now—is always there—flat on the ground, flat on his face, wishing he were dead.

There is a rising murmur of excited voices at the gate.

Now what's all that noise about?

AGLAIA *comes hurriedly out of the palace.*

36

AGLAIA:

What's all that noise? Watchman, how can you allow that noise?

WATCHMAN:

> *Hobbling to the gate.*

They've only just begun it.

AGLAIA:

> *At the gate.*

What's all this cackling about? Don't you know you must be quiet?

WATCHMAN:

Have you no sense? Have you no hearts? What? What?

AGLAIA:

What? What messenger? Tell him to go around to the front of the palace and to go quietly. What messenger? Where's he from?

> *Enter* ALCESTIS, *from the palace.*

ALCESTIS:

There must be no noise. There must be no noise. Aglaia, how can you allow this noise?

AGLAIA:

Queen Alcestis, they say that a messenger has come.

ALCESTIS:

What messenger?

WATCHMAN:

> *Has received through the gate a small rectangular leaf of gold, which he gives to* ALCESTIS.

They are saying that a messenger came during the night and left this.

ALCESTIS *stands looking at it in her hand. The* WATCHMAN *leans over and examines it in her hand and continues talking officiously.*

It is of gold, lady. See, those are the signs—that is the writing—of the Southland. There is the sun . . . and the tripod . . . and the laurel. . . . Queen Alcestis, it is from Delphi. It is a message from Delphi!

ALCESTIS *suddenly performs the ritual: she places the leaf first to her forehead, then on her heart, then on her lips.*

ALCESTIS:

Where is the messenger?

The WATCHMAN *goes to the gate—now slightly open—and holds a whispered colloquy.*

WATCHMAN:

Turning back toward ALCESTIS.

He went away—hours ago, they say.

ALCESTIS:

Who can read this writing? Watchman, go call those four herdsmen!

WATCHMAN:

They are here, lady—all four of them.

Again a busy colloquy at the gate. It opens further to admit the four HERDSMEN. *The* HERDSMAN *who held the long conversation with* ALCESTIS *in Act I flings himself on the ground, face downward, holding his head in his hands.*

ALCESTIS:

Can one of you read the writing of the Southland?

HERDSMAN:

> *Raising his head.*

I can . . . a little, Queen Alcestis.

ALCESTIS:

Then stand. Stand up.

> *He rises. She puts the leaf in his hand. He looks at it a moment, then puts it to his forehead, heart, and lips; and says in awe:*

HERDSMAN:

It is from the temple of Apollo at Delphi.

> *Some* TOWNSPEOPLE *have pressed through the gate. The* HERDSMAN *starts reading with great difficulty.*

"Peace . . . and long life . . . to Admetus the Hospitable, King of Thessaly, rich in horses."

ALCESTIS:

Long life?

HERDSMAN:

"Peace and long life to Admetus the Hospitable—"

ALCESTIS:

Stop.

> *To the* WATCHMAN.

Close the gate.

> *The* WATCHMAN *pushes the* TOWNSPEOPLE *off the stage, and after a glance at* ALCESTIS, *also drives off the three other* HERDSMEN. *He closes the gate.* ALCESTIS *returns to the reader, who has been trying to decipher the text.*

HERDSMAN:

"King Admetus . . . *not* . . . will not . . . die."

AGLAIA:

Great is Apollo! Great is Apollo!

HERDSMAN:

"Will not die . . . if . . . if . . . because . . . no, if . . . another . . . if someone else . . . if a second person . . . desires . . .
> *He points to his heart.*

wishes . . . longs . . . desires to die . . ." Lady, I do not know this last word.

ALCESTIS:

I know it.

HERDSMAN:

> *Struggling, finds it.*

"In his place . . . in his stead." Great is Apollo!

AGLAIA:

What does it say? What does it say?

WATCHMAN:

I. I shall die.
> *Starting left.*

My sword, where is my sword?

AGLAIA:

> *Getting the idea.*

No.
> *Strongly, to the* WATCHMAN.

No. This message is for me. I was there when he was born: I shall die for him. I shall throw myself in the river.

WATCHMAN:

> *Returning; to* AGLAIA.

This is not for a woman to do.

40

HERDSMAN:

> *Kneeling, his fists pressed against his eyes in concentration.*

I have begun to die already.

AGLAIA:

Queen Alcestis, tell me . . . I must do it properly: how does one die for King Admetus?

WATCHMAN:

> *Self-importantly, placing himself between* AGLAIA *and* ALCESTIS.

Give your orders to me, Queen Alcestis. It is very clear that this message was meant for me.

HERDSMAN:

> *Again throwing himself full length on the ground.*

I struck him. I am to blame for all!

ALCESTIS:

> *Who has waited, motionless, for silence.*

How would you die in his stead?

> *Pause.*

Do you think it is enough to fling yourself into the river—or to run a sword through your heart?

> *Pause.*

No—the gods do not ask what is easy of us, but what is difficult.

AGLAIA:

> *Sobbing.*

Queen Alcestis, how does one die for King Admetus?

HERDSMAN:

I know. I know.

> *He turns and starts to go to the gate.*

Peace and long life to King Admetus!

ALCESTIS:

> *To the* HERDSMAN.

Wait!

> *They all watch her. She says quietly:*

Aglaia, go and lay out the dress in which I was married.

AGLAIA:

> *Stares at her in sudden realization; horrified whisper.*

No. No . . . you must not . . .

ALCESTIS:

Tell the children I am coming to see them. Tell the King the sun is warm here. He must come out and sit in it.

> *Sudden clamor from the others.*

AGLAIA:

No. No, Queen Alcestis. We are old. Our lives are over.

WATCHMAN:

Lady, look at me—I am an old man.

AGLAIA:

You cannot do this. He would not wish it. You are queen; you are mother.

ALCESTIS:

> *Restraining their noise by voice and gesture.*

First! First I order you to say nothing of this to anyone. Aglaia, do you hear me?

AGLAIA:

Yes, Queen Alcestis.

ALCESTIS:

Watchman!

WATCHMAN:
Yes, Queen Alcestis.

ALCESTIS:
To no one—until tomorrow. No matter what takes place here, you will show no surprise, no grief. Now leave me alone with this man.

> *Pointing to the* HERDSMAN.
> AGLAIA *goes into the palace; the* WATCHMAN *out left.*
> *The* HERDSMAN *stands with one fist on his forehead in concentration, and suddenly cries:*

HERDSMAN:
King Admetus—rise up! Rise up!

ALCESTIS:
You cannot save him.

HERDSMAN:
I have begun to die already.

ALCESTIS:
Yes, maybe you could do it. But you would do it imperfectly. You wish to die, yes . . . not for love of Admetus, but to lift the burden of that crime from off your heart. This is work of love, Herdsman; not work of expiation, but of love.

HERDSMAN:
> *Almost angrily.*
I, too, love Admetus.

ALCESTIS:
Who does not love Admetus? But your death would be a small death. You long to die: I dread, fear, hate to die. I must die from Admetus—

She looks upward.

from this sunlight. Only so will he be restored. Can you give him that?

He is silent. She continues, as though talking to herself.

I know now what I have to do and how to do it. But I do not know why . . . why this has been asked of me. You . . . you can help me to understand why I must die.

HERDSMAN:

I?

ALCESTIS:

Yes, you—who came from Delphi; in whom Apollo—

HERDSMAN:

In sincere repudiation.

Lady . . . Princess, I told you—again and again. If Apollo was in us herdsmen, he was not in me!

ALCESTIS:

Softly and lightly.

You made clear to me that Apollo willed my marriage.

HERDSMAN:

Still almost angrily.

No. No. You asked me questions. I answered as any man would answer. You know well that I am an ordinary man.

ALCESTIS *turns in suffering frustration toward the palace door; then turns back again to the* HERDSMAN.

ALCESTIS:

Then speak again as an ordinary man, and tell me why Apollo asks me to die.

HERDSMAN:

Still with a touch of anger.

44

Then as an ordinary man I answer you—as many an ordinary man would: Delphi has said that one of us must die. I am ready to die. Why should I try to understand it?

ALCESTIS:

But if we do not understand, our lives are little better than those of the animals.

HERDSMAN:

No! Princess, to understand means to see the whole of a thing. Do we men ever see the whole of a story, the end of a story? If you let me die now for Admetus, I would not know what followed after my death, but I would die willingly. For I have always seen that there are two kinds of death: one which is an end; and one which is a going forward, which is big with what follows after it. And I would know that a death which had been laid on me by Delphi would be a death which led on to something. For if the gods exist, that is their sign: that whatever they do is an unfolding—a part of something larger than we can see. Let me die this death, Princess —for it would save me from that other death which I dread and which all men dread: the mere ceasing to be; the dust in the grave.

> ALCESTIS *has received his words as full answer and solution.*
> *Her mood changes; she says lightly and quickly:*

ALCESTIS:

No, Herdsman, live—live for Admetus, for me, and for my children. Are you not the friend of Epimenes—he who hates you now because you struck his father? You have almost broken his heart. He thought you were his friend—you who taught him to swim and to fish. Before I go I shall tell Epimenes that you have done me a great kindness.

In silence the HERDSMAN *goes out the gate.*
ALCESTIS *again makes the ritual gesture with the gold leaf—forehead, heart, lips. Enter* AGLAIA *from the palace.*

AGLAIA:

With lowered head.
The dress is ready, Queen Alcestis.

ALCESTIS:

Aglaia, for what I have to do now I cannot—I must not—see the children. Their heads smell so sweet. Do you understand?

AGLAIA:

Yes, Queen Alcestis.

ALCESTIS:

You are to tell Epimenes—from me—that he is to go to the herdsman who struck his father . . . that he is to forgive him, and to thank him for a great kindness which he has done me.

AGLAIA:

I shall tell him.

ALCESTIS:

You are to cut a lock of my hair. Say nothing to anyone, and place it on the altar
Pointing to the gate.
in the grove of Apollo, across the road. Aglaia, after I am gone, you are to tell King Admetus that I have said that I wish him to marry again.

AGLAIA:

Queen Alcestis!

ALCESTIS:

A man must have that comfort. But oh, Aglaia! They say that stepmothers often bear ill will toward the children of the former

wife. Stay by them! Stay near them! And oh, Aglaia—from time
to time recall me to him.

Her voice breaking.

Recall me to him!

She rushes into the palace.

*AGLAIA is about to follow when she is stopped by excited
whispering and talking at the gate. Some TOWNSPEOPLE
take a few steps into the court. RHODOPE, a young girl of
the palace servants, smothering her happy giggling, runs from
the gate to the palace door.*

AGLAIA:

What is this? What is this noise? Rhodope!

RHODOPE:

He's coming along the road!

AGLAIA:

Who?

RHODOPE and TOWNSPEOPLE:

Hercules is coming! He's down the valley! Hercules, son of
Zeus!

AGLAIA:

Hush, all of you. Go out of the court. Have you forgotten that
there is sickness in this house! Rhodope, go in the house and hold
your tongue!

*TOWNSPEOPLE disappear. RHODOPE slips through the palace
door as it is opened by the WATCHMAN, who enters, preceding two SERVANTS, who are not yet seen with the day bed.
Then to AGLAIA, whose head is lowered in anxiety.*

WATCHMAN:

Hercules! Today of all days!

47

AGLAIA:

> *In a bad humor.*

Yes. Yes. And every year. Why does he come every year? Do we know?

WATCHMAN:

But . . . so great a friend!

AGLAIA:

Yes, but great friends can sometimes make us a present of their absence.

WATCHMAN:

Aglaia, I don't understand you!

AGLAIA:

> *Irritably.*

I know what I know.

> *From the palace come two* SERVANTS. *They are bearing a day bed and a low stool.*

WATCHMAN:

> *To the* SERVANTS.

Come on . . . put them down here. You know where.

AGLAIA:

> *Taking over the ordering, while the* WATCHMAN *turns back to help* ADMETUS.

Here, right here!

> *Getting her bearings by the sun.*

Turn it so.

> *She takes the cushions from them.*

So. There. And the Queen likes to sit here.

> *Enter* ADMETUS, *supported, his arms around the shoulders of the* WATCHMAN *and a* GUARD.

ADMETUS:

The sun is already halfway up the sky.

> *To the* WATCHMAN.

You have watched all night. You should be asleep.

WATCHMAN:

Oh, we old men, King Admetus, we sleep very little. Gently. Gently now.

ADMETUS:

I don't know where the Queen is, Aglaia.

AGLAIA:

> *Busies herself with the cushions.*

She'll be here in a minute, King Admetus. You can be sure of that.

> *She goes quickly into the palace.*

WATCHMAN:

Now, sire, when you're comfortably settled on that couch, I have some news for you. You'll scarcely believe it.

> *He squints up at the sun.*

Yes, sire, it will be a very hot day. We are in the solstice. The sailors say that the sun swings low, that He is very near us these days. That's what they say.

ADMETUS:

What is your news?

WATCHMAN:

A great friend, sire, is coming to see you—a very good friend.

ADMETUS:

Hercules!

WATCHMAN:

Yes, Hercules, son of Zeus!

ADMETUS:

Today! Today of all days!

WATCHMAN:

The whole town knows it. Oh, he comes slowly enough. At every village, every farm, they bring him wine; they put garlands on his head. He is very drunk. . . . Oh, King Admetus, we must prevent his embracing you. You remember his embraces. He would surely kill you today.

ADMETUS:

Does the Queen know?

WATCHMAN:

Oh, the maids will have told her all about it.

ADMETUS:

I wish he could have come at another time.

WATCHMAN:

Every time is a good time for Hercules. Your sons, sire, are beside themselves. Epimenes will ask him all over again how he killed the Nemean lion and how he cleaned the stables of King Augeas.

ADMETUS:

Call Aglaia.

> Enter AGLAIA *from the palace door.*

WATCHMAN:

Here she is now.

AGLAIA:

Yes, King Admetus?

Behind the KING'S *back, with her hand she directs the* WATCHMAN *to leave. He exits left.*

ADMETUS:

Aglaia—come near to me. You have heard the news?
    The WATCHMAN *as he leaves gives* AGLAIA *an anxious look and is relieved by her answer.*

AGLAIA:

Yes, I have: the son of Zeus is coming to visit us.

ADMETUS:

    Without pathos.
Aglaia, this is my last day. I know it. I feel it.

AGLAIA:

Sire, how would any of us know that? You must not talk now. You must save your strength.

ADMETUS:

I shall die before sundown. Now, if it is possible—and you must make it possible—my death must be hidden from Hercules, for at least a day or two. You must say that one of the servants has died. And you must go about your life as though nothing had happened. The Queen will show you the way of it. You know what Hercules's life is like—those great labors, one after another. When he comes to us as a happy visitor, we would not wish to show him a house of mourning. Especially Hercules, who is so often on the point of losing his life, and who has such an aversion to all that has to do with burial and mourning.

AGLAIA:

    Again arranging his cushions.
King Admetus, I am not a fool. All these things I understand very well. Now lie back and shut your eyes. This sunlight is going to give you strength.

51

ADMETUS:

If it could only give me strength for one more day—to welcome Hercules! Go and see where the Queen is.

AGLAIA:

Here she is.

> *Exit* AGLAIA *left.*
> *Enter* ALCESTIS *from the palace door. She stands on the top step. She is wearing the dress of Act I.* ADMETUS *turns and gazes at her in silence.*

ADMETUS:

Our wedding dress!

ALCESTIS:

> *Smiling, puts her finger on her lips to silence him; she goes to him and says lightly:*

Most wives save it for their burial. I wear it for life.

ADMETUS:

Sit here, dearest. I was just saying to Aglaia—

> ALCESTIS *sits on the stool beside* ADMETUS *and rests her hand beside his.*

ALCESTIS:

Yes, yes, I know—when Hercules comes . . .

ADMETUS:

He will soon be here.

ALCESTIS:

Oh, he is being detained on the road. Hercules goes quickly only to danger. Perhaps he will be here tonight . . . perhaps not till tomorrow. We have time.

> *She rises and goes to the center of the stage and stands there listening.*

52

I hear shouts of joy in the valley.

She walks slowly back to her stool and repeats:

We have time.

In the center of the stage, gazing at the sun as if for help.

This is the healing sun—the sun of the summer solstice. Do you feel it?

ADMETUS:

It is the healing sun, but for others. I have put all that behind me: I do not need hope. My life was short, but a single hour can hold the whole fullness of time. The fullness of time was given to me. A man who has been happy is no longer the subject of time. . . . Come, we'll say to each other what is still to be said on this last day.

ALCESTIS:

Returning to her place beside him; with a gentle smile.

This last day? You must rest and save your strength and breath. I shall talk. I shall talk for two—for you and for me. I do not know who gave me that second name: Alcestis the Silent. I think it was you, but also it was Hercules who carried it over Greece.

ADMETUS:

Were you always silent?

ALCESTIS:

I? No. As a girl—oh, I was a contentious and argumentative girl, as you know well. But there are times when I am impatient with my silence—this tiresome, silent Alcestis! There are times when I wish to be like other women, who can freely say what is in their hearts. What do other wives say? I think they must say something like this: Admetus . . . have I ever told you—let me look into your eyes again—have I ever told you that I have loved you more than life itself?

> *Leaning over him, she is suddenly stricken with great pain. She rises, whirls about, one hand to her head, the other to her left side, where his wound is.* ADMETUS *has not noticed it. He has closed his eyes again, and starts to laugh in a low, long murmur.*

ADMETUS:

That does not sound . . . no, that does not sound like my silent Alcestis. And if you were to speak for me, what would you say?

ALCESTIS:

> *The pain has slackened and she replies almost serenely.*

I would say that I—I, Admetus—have chosen neither the day of my birth nor the day of my death. That having been born is a gift that fell to our lot—a wonderful gift—and that Alcestis's death—or my own—comes from the same hand.

ADMETUS:

> *Almost amused.*

Your death, Alcestis?

ALCESTIS:

Were it to come from the same hand that gives life . . . Are you in pain, Admetus?

ADMETUS:

> *Puts his hand to his side wonderingly.*

No. I do not know why it is, but the pain seems to have . . .

ALCESTIS:

Lift your hand!

> *As he slowly raises his paralyzed left hand, the pain passes into her body; she clutches her side, bending in agony.*

ADMETUS:

This lightness!

He stares before him with hope.

No, I must not think of such things. I have put that behind me. We who have known what we have known . . . are not the subjects of time.

ALCESTIS:

The great pain has passed, but she moves guardedly; she has sat down again and speaks with her cheek pressed close to his.

Yes, we, who were happy . . .

ADMETUS:

Suddenly grasping her hand, ardently.

And you hated me once!

ALCESTIS:

Withdrawing her hand.

No, never.

ADMETUS:

That young man who kept coming back to that trial of the lion and the boar . . . There he is again—that young idiot from Thessaly.

They are both laughing.

ALCESTIS:

Oh, what a road I have come!

ADMETUS:

You didn't hate me, as I came around the corner straining over those damned beasts?

ALCESTIS:

No. I suffered the more for it. I had begun to love that stern-faced young man from Thessaly. You were the only suitor who attempted that trial twice. . . . Even Hercules gave up. . . . To think that I could not see where life was carrying me!

ADMETUS:
Proudly, ardently.
I, I saw.

ALCESTIS:
Beloved Admetus . . . you saw. You married this self-willed, obstinate girl.

ADMETUS:
More ardently.
Our love! Our love! . . . Our whisperings in the night! . . . The birth of Epimenes, when I almost lost you . . .
She makes gestures of trying to silence him.
Alcestis! What we have known, what we have lived . . . Oh, to live forever—with you—beside you.

ALCESTIS:
Ssh! There are things that we human beings are not permitted to say aloud.

ADMETUS:
Tentatively putting his foot on the ground.
I do not understand. . . . My knee does not tremble.
With joyous hope.
Alcestis! It may be . . . it may be I shall live.

ALCESTIS:
Equally ecstatic, to the sky.
Living or dead, we are watched; we are guided; we are understood. Oh, Admetus, lie quiet, lie still!

ADMETUS:
I dare not . . . believe . . . hope . . .

ALCESTIS:

The pain returns; she is starting toward the palace door.
Admetus, I would find it a natural thing, if a message came
from Delphi to me, saying that I should give my life for my
children or for Thessaly or . . . for my husband—

ADMETUS:

No. No. No man would wish another to die for him. Every man
is ready to die his own death.

ALCESTIS:

Mastering her suffering.
What are you saying, Admetus? Think of all the soldiers—
thousands and thousands of them—who have died for others.
And we women, poor cowardly soldiers, have died—a great
many of us—for our husbands and children.
She starts stumbling toward the palace door.

ADMETUS:

I would think less of the gods who could lay such a decision
between husband and wife. . . .
Rising; in loud amazement.
Look! This lightness!

ALCESTIS:

Aglaia! Aglaia!

ADMETUS:

Springs up and rushes to her.
Alcestis, you are in trouble! Aglaia! Aglaia!
AGLAIA *hurries to her from the palace door.*

ALCESTIS:

Take me to my bed.

ADMETUS:

You are ill. Are you ill, Alcestis?

ALCESTIS:

> *Turning.*

Take my life. Be happy. Be happy.

> *She collapses in their arms and is carried into the palace. From beyond the gate come sounds of an excited crowd, fragments of singing, etc., and the roar of* HERCULES'S *voice.*

HERCULES:

Where is my old friend Ad-meeee-tus?

TOWNSPEOPLE:

Hercules is here! Hercules is here!

HERCULES:

Al-cess-s-stis! Where is the divine Al-cess-stis? Alcestis the Silent! Admetus the Hoss-s-spitable!

> *The* WATCHMAN *enters.*

TOWNSPEOPLE:

Hercules is here! Hercules!

WATCHMAN:

The gods preserve us! What can be done?

> *More* TOWNSPEOPLE *pour in the gate, shouting, "Long live Hercules, son of Zeus!" Enter* HERCULES—*drunk, happy, garlanded—a jug in his hand. Two* VILLAGERS *laughingly carry* HERCULES'S *club as a great burden.*

HERCULES:

Alcestis, fairest of the daughters of Iolcos! Admetus, crown of friends! Where are they?

TOWNSPEOPLE:

Hercules, the destroyer of beasts! Hercules, the friend of man! Long live Hercules!

WATCHMAN:

Welcome a thousand times to Pherai, great Hercules!

HERCULES:

Where is my friend Epimenes—the mighty hunter, the mighty fisherman? Epimenes, I shall wrestle with you. By the God's thunder, you shall not throw me again!

WATCHMAN:

All of them will be here in a minute, Hercules. They are beside themselves with joy.

A wailing, a keening, is heard in the palace.

HERCULES:

That's weeping I hear. What is that wailing, old man?

WATCHMAN:

Wailing, Hercules! The women and girls are rejoicing that Hercules has come.

Enter AGLAIA *in haste from the palace.*

AGLAIA:

A thousand times welcome, divine Hercules. The King and Queen will be here in a moment. Happy, happy they are—you can be sure of that. Oh, son of Zeus, what a joy to see you!

HERCULES:

Loudly.

I'm not the son of Zeus!

AGLAIA:

Covering her ears.

Hercules, what are you saying?

HERCULES:

I'm the son of Amphytrion and Alcmene. I'm a common man, Aglaia; and the work I do is as hard for me as for any other.

AGLAIA:

Oh, may the gods prevent misfortune from coming to this house! You're very drunk, Hercules, to say such a wicked thing as that.

HERCULES:

I'm a man, just an ordinary man, I tell you.

AGLAIA:

God or man, Hercules, what do I see? Hercules, you are filthy! Is this the handsomest man in all Greece? By the immortal gods, I would never have known you! Now listen: you remember the baths that Aglaia prepares? They'd take the skin off an ordinary man. And the oil I have ready for you—you remember the oil, don't you?

HERCULES:

> *Confidentially.*

First, Aglaia—first!

> *He makes a gesture of drinking.*

AGLAIA:

You haven't forgotten our wine, is that it? You shall have some immediately!

HERCULES:

> *Suddenly roaring.*

On the road they told me that Admetus had been stabbed and wounded. Who struck him, Aglaia?

AGLAIA:

Oh, that's all forgotten, Hercules. He's as well now as you or I!

RHODOPE *and another* GIRL *come from the palace bearing a wine jar and some cups.*

Come, sit here and refresh yourself.

HERCULES *tries to catch one of the girls, who eludes him. He then starts in pursuit of the other. He catches her.*

HERCULES:

What's your name, little pigeon?

AGLAIA:

Angrily.

Hercules!

The GIRL *escapes.* HERCULES *runs after her, stumbles, and falls flat on the ground.*

HERCULES:

Oh! I've hurt myself! Hell and confusion! My knee! My knee!

AGLAIA:

Hercules! I haven't one bit of pity for you. Can you have forgotten where you are? Immortal heavens, what would Queen Alcestis think—you behaving like that!

HERCULES:

Who has slowly got up and sat down.

Twenty days I've walked. Where are they? Where are my friends, Admetus and Alcestis?

AGLAIA:

Confidentially.

Now, Hercules, you're an old friend of the house, aren't you?

HERCULES:

I am!

AGLAIA:

We can talk quite plainly to you, can't we? You're not one of those guests we have to conceal things from, thank the gods!

HERCULES:

I'm their brother! Their brother!

AGLAIA:

Now listen: one of the women in the house, an orphan . . . one of the women in the house . . .

HERCULES:

What? Dead?

AGLAIA:

Finger on lips.

And you know how loyal and kind King Admetus and Queen Alcestis are to all of us who serve here. . . .

HERCULES:

Dead? An orphan?

AGLAIA:

Yes, she'd lost both her father and mother. Now, they'll be here in just a minute—after you've had your bath. But now, just now —you know: they are by that poor girl, in friendship and piety. You understand everything, Hercules?

HERCULES:

No. No, Aglaia, there are too many things I do not understand. But do you know who understands them all?

Pause.

Alcestis. Am I not right, Aglaia?

AGLAIA:

Yes. Yes, Hercules.

HERCULES:

Now I am going to talk frankly to you, Aglaia: I have come here —I have walked twenty days—to ask Alcestis one question.

AGLAIA:

A question, Hercules?

> *For answer,* HERCULES *twice points quickly and emphatically toward the zenith.*

About the gods?

> *He nods.* AGLAIA *recovers herself and says briskly:*

Well, first you must have that bath. You will come out of it looking like a boy of seventeen. And I have such a garland for you. And such perfumes!

> *He rises and starts to follow her to the palace steps.*

HERCULES:

And while I'm taking the bath you will sit beside me and tell me again how Apollo came to Thessaly?

AGLAIA:

Yes, I will. I'll tell you once more.

HERCULES:

> *Stopping her; with urgency.*

And no one knew which was Apollo?

> *She shakes her head.*

A whole year, and no one knew which was Apollo—not even Alcestis?

> *Again she shakes her head.* HERCULES *clutches his forehead.*

Aglaia, who can understand them? We shall never understand them. When I try to think of them, I start trembling; I get dizzy.

AGLAIA:

Hercules! You are tired. Come. . . .

Enter ADMETUS. *He stands at the top of the stairs as* HERCULES *and* AGLAIA *reach the bottom step.*

ADMETUS:
Loudly.
Welcome, Hercules, friend of all men; Hercules, benefactor of all men!

HERCULES:
Admetus! Old friend!
ADMETUS *puts his hands on* HERCULES'S *shoulders. They gaze into one another's eyes.*

ADMETUS:
From where have you come, Hercules?

HERCULES:
From labors, Admetus . . . from labors.

AGLAIA:
King Admetus, Hercules's bath is ready. You can begin talking when he comes out.
Looking up.
It will be evening soon.

ADMETUS:
No, first we will drink a bowl of wine together! Come, sit down, Hercules. For a short time I was ill, and this foolish womanish couch is where I used to sit in the sun. Now tell me—what has been your latest great labor?
AGLAIA *and the* GIRLS *have gone into the palace.*

HERCULES:
Hushed, wide-eyed.
Admetus, Admetus—I killed the Hydra.

64

ADMETUS:

> *Rising, in awed astonishment.*

Great-hearted Hercules! You slew the Hydra! By the immortal gods, Hercules, you are the friend of man. Slew the Hydra! The Hydra!

HERCULES:

> *Beckoning to* ADMETUS *to draw his face nearer for a confidence.*

Admetus—

> *Again beckoning.*

It wasn't easy!

ADMETUS:

I can well believe it!

HERCULES:

> *Almost bitterly; gazing into his face.*

It was not easy.

> *Abrupt change to urgent earnestness.*

Admetus, am I the son of Zeus?

ADMETUS:

Hercules! Everyone knows that you are the son of Zeus and Alcmene.

HERCULES:

One person can tell me. That is what I have come to ask Alcestis. Where is Alcestis, queen of women?

ADMETUS:

But Aglaia told you!

HERCULES:

Oh, yes. Who is this orphan girl that has died? Was she one of the first in the house?

ADMETUS:

She called herself the servant of the servants.

HERCULES:

But you were all fond of her?

ADMETUS:

Yes. We all loved her.

HERCULES:

You see, Admetus, everyone says I am the son of Zeus and there-
fore my labors must be easier for me than for another man. If I
have the blood and the heart and the lungs of Him

> *Pointing upward.*

in me, shouldn't they be easy? But, Admetus, they are not
easy. The Hydra!

> *He wraps his arms around Admetus in imitation of a snake
> and sets his face in extreme horror.*

I was about to burst. The blood sprang out of my ears like
fountains. If I am only a man—the son of Amphytrion and
Alcmene—then, Admetus,

> *Peering into* ADMETUS's *face with strained urgency.*

then I'm a very good man!

ADMETUS:

God or man, Hercules—god or man, all men honor and are
grateful to you.

HERCULES:

But I want to know. Some days I feel that I am the son of Zeus.
Other days I am . . . I am a beast, Admetus, a beast and a brute.
Every month messengers arrive from all over Greece, asking me
to come and do this and do that. I'll do no more; I won't do a
single thing until I've settled this matter. One of these days—yes,
I foresee it—someone will come to me and ask me to . . . descend

into the underworld . . . into Hell, Admetus, and bring back someone who has died.

Rising, in terrified repudiation.

No! No! *That* I will not do. God or man, *no one* may ask that of me!

ADMETUS:

Sincerely shocked.

No, Hercules—that has never been done, nor even thought of.

HERCULES:

Every time I come here I look at that—that entrance to Hell— with great fear, Admetus.

ADMETUS:

You must not think such thoughts!

HERCULES:

Even a son of Zeus couldn't do that, could he? So—so do you see the question? Isn't that an important question? And who can answer it? Who is wisest in just these matters where you and I are most ignorant? You know who: she who never speaks, or speaks so little. The Silent. She is silent, isn't she?

ADMETUS:

Yes, she is silent.

HERCULES:

But she'll speak to me . . . to her old friend Hercules? She'll speak for me, won't she?

He pours himself more wine.

Do you know, Admetus—do you know what your Alcestis is?

ADMETUS, *in pain, rises, and sits down.*

No, you don't know. I journey from place to place—from court to court. I've seen them all—the queens and princesses

67

of Greece. The daughters of the men we knew and the girls we courted are growing up. Oedipus of Thebes has a daughter, Antigone; and there is Penelope, who's just married the son of Laertes of Ithaca. Leda of Sparta has two daughters, Helen and Clytemnestra. I've seen 'em all, talked to 'em all. What are they beside Alcestis? Dirt. Trash.

> AGLAIA *comes from the palace bearing a garland of vine leaves. The* WATCHMAN *follows with a jar of oil. They stand listening.*
>
> HERCULES *rises and, in drunken energy close to violence, turns* ADMETUS *about, shouting.*

Do you know? Do you know to the full?

ADMETUS:
> *In agony, raising his arms.*

I know, Hercules.

HERCULES:

Do you know all—her power to forgive, to pardon? No, you don't know a thing. Alcestis is the crown of Greece. The crown of women.

ADMETUS:
> *Taking three steps backward.*

Hercules! Alcestis is dead.
> *Pause.*

The servant of servants. Forgive us, Hercules!

HERCULES:
> *Silence. A great rage rises in him. Then with savage bitterness.*

Admetus . . . you are no friend. By the immortal gods, you are my worst enemy!

He grasps him by the throat and, walking backward, drags the unresisting ADMETUS *with him.*

If you were not Admetus, I would kill you now!

AGLAIA and WATCHMAN:

Hercules! Hercules, Queen Alcestis wished it! She wanted us not to tell you until later.

HERCULES:

You have treated me as no friend. I thought I was your brother.

AGLAIA:

Pounding with her fists on his back.

Hercules! Hercules!

HERCULES:

Alcestis dead—and I was not worthy to be told! You let me boast and drink and revel . . .

AGLAIA:

It was her wish, Hercules. Alcestis commanded it.

HERCULES:

Broodingly, holding ADMETUS *bent far backward before him.*

You think I have no mind or heart or soul. What do I care for the thanks and praise of the world if I am not fit to share the grief of my friends?

Pause.

AGLAIA:

It was for hospitality, Hercules. She wished it!

HERCULES:

Hospitality is for guests, not brothers.

ADMETUS:

> *Quietly.*

Forgive us, Hercules.

HERCULES:

> *Releasing* ADMETUS.

Alcestis is dead. Alcestis is in the underworld.

> *Suddenly struck by an idea; loudly.*

In Hell! Where is my club? My club! I shall go and get her!

AGLAIA:

Hercules!

ADMETUS:

No, Hercules. Live! She died in my place. She died for me. It is not right that still another die.

HERCULES:

My club! My club! Admetus, now I shall tell you something—something that no man knows. Now all the world may know it.

> *He has advanced to the top of the path.*

I once came near to Alcestis in violence, in brutish violence. Yes, I, Hercules, son of Zeus, did that! A god—some god—intervened in time, to save her and to save me. Alcestis forgave me. How can that be? How can any man understand that? She spoke of it to no one in the world. And when I came to Pherai there was no sign in her face, in her eyes, that I had been the criminal. Only a god can understand that—only that loving smile. Forgiveness is not within our power—we commoner men. Only the strong and pure can forgive. I never wanted that she should forget that evil moment—no!—for in her remembering it lay my happiness; for her remembering and her forgiving were one.

ADMETUS:

Hercules, I shall come with you.

HERCULES:

Stay and rule, Admetus. Your labors I cannot do; you cannot do mine. What god shall I call on? Not my father—father and no father. Who is the god you mainly worship here?

AGLAIA:

Have you forgotten, Hercules? This is Apollo's land.

HERCULES:

Yes, now I remember. I have had little to do with Him, but . . .
Looking to heaven.
Apollo, I am Hercules, called the son of Zeus and Alcmene. All Greece says that you have loved these two—Admetus and Alcestis. You know what I'm about to do. You know I can't do it by myself. Put into my arm a strength that's never been there before. You do this—or let's say, you and I do this together. And if we can do it, let everybody see that a new knowledge has been given to us of what gods and men can do together.

ADMETUS:

One moment, Hercules.
He goes down the path.
Pytho! Pytho! This is Hercules, the loved friend of Alcestis and of me and of Epimenes. Let him pass, Pytho—going and coming.

HERCULES:

Go into the palace, Admetus—all of you. I must work as I must live—alone.
It is dark. The characters on the stage withdraw, except for

71

ADMETUS, *who stands by the palace door, covering his face with his cloak. A low beating on tympani, like distant thunder, grows louder, strikes a sharp blow, and jumps up a fourth.* HERCULES *has disappeared into the door of the cave. Presently he returns, leading* ALCESTIS. *Over her white dress and head she wears a dark veil, which trails many yards behind her. As they reach the stage,* HERCULES *releases her hand. She sways, with groping steps, as though drugged with sleep.* HERCULES *shoulders his club and goes off in his solitary way.* ADMETUS, *holding his cloak before him, as before a strong light, approaches, enfolds her. She rests her head on his breast. He leads her into the palace.*

ACT III

Twelve years later. Again, first streaks of dawn.
Enter left, ALCESTIS—*old, broken, in rags. She is carrying a*
water jar. She descends to the spring to fill it.
Noise of a crowd on the road.

TOWNSPEOPLE:
Outside the palace gates.
King Agis, help us! Save us! . . . King Agis must help us. . . . We
want to talk to King Agis!
Enter hurriedly, in horrified protest, a new and younger NIGHT
WATCHMAN. *He also carries a lighted lantern and a rattle. His*
face is smeared with ashes. He opens the gate a crack and speaks
through it.

WATCHMAN:
You know the order: anyone who puts foot in these gates will be
killed.

TOWNSPEOPLE:
Pressing in and overrunning the WATCHMAN.
Let him kill us! We're dying already! . . . The King must do
something.

WATCHMAN:
Looking over his shoulder toward the palace, in terror.
The King's doing everything he can. Pestilences and plagues
come from the gods, he says, and only the gods can stop them.

73

Bury your dead, he says, bury them the moment they fall. And smear your faces with ashes; rub your whole body with ashes and cinders. That way the plague can't see you, he says, and it will pass you by.

TOWNSPEOPLE:
We've heard all that before. We want to see Queen Alcestis. Queen Alcestis! She can help us. Queen Alcestis!

WATCHMAN:
> *Indignantly.*

What do you mean—Queen Alcestis? There's no Queen Alcestis here. She's a slave, and the lowest of the slaves!

> ALCESTIS *has come up the path, her jar on her shoulder. She stands and listens. The* WATCHMAN *sees her.*

There she is!

> *Violently.*

Look at her! *She* brought the plague. She *is* the plague. It's she that's brought the curse on Thessaly!

TOWNSPEOPLE:
> *After a shocked silence, an outburst of contradictory cries.*

No, never! Not Queen Alcestis! What did he say? How did she bring it?

ALCESTIS:
> *Her head turning slowly as she looks into their faces; barely a question.*

I—brought the plague? I brought the plague?

WATCHMAN:
She was dead, wasn't she? And Hercules brought her back from death, didn't he? She brought back death with her. Everybody belonging to her is dead. Her husband killed. Two of her children killed. One of her sons got away—but who's heard of him

74

for a dozen years? The King will have her killed or driven from the country.

ALCESTIS:

No, I did not bring this disease to Thessaly. Take me to these judges. If it is I who have brought misfortune to Thessaly, let them take my life and remove the disease from you and your children.

> ALCESTIS *moves off to the left, into the servants' quarters.*
> *Light slowly comes up on* APOLLO, *standing on the roof.*

TOWNSPEOPLE:

No! She could not have brought evil to Thessaly! That is Alcestis the Wise!

WATCHMAN:

> *Amid contradictory cries from the* CROWD.

Go to your homes! You'll all be killed here.

> *To those in front.*

What do you know about it? Ignorant boors! Away, all of you! I've warned you. You know what kind of man King Agis is.

> TOWNSPEOPLE *disappear, murmuring and grumbling, through the palace gate. The* WATCHMAN *goes off left, shaking his rattle. As he goes:*

Dawn . . . dawn . . . and all is well in the palace of Agis, King of Thessaly, rich in horses. . . .

> DEATH *comes out of the cave, ascends the path, and sniffs at the doors.*

APOLLO:

Death!

DEATH:

> *Who hasn't noticed Him; taken unawares.*

Ah, you're here again!

APOLLO:

It is getting light. You are shuddering.

DEATH:

Yes. Yes, but I have some questions to ask you. Lord Apollo, I can't understand what you mean by this. So many dead! Down where I live there's such a crowding and trampling and waiting in line! And never have I seen so many children! But I confess to you, Lord Apollo, I don't know what you mean by it: you are the God of healing—of life and of healing—and here you are, the sender of plagues and pestilence. You loved Admetus, and his family, and his people; and all you do is kill them.

APOLLO:

A smile.

I loved Alcestis, and I killed her—once.

DEATH:

Contemptible, what you did!

APOLLO:

Have you mended the wall—that wall through which Hercules broke?

DEATH:

Broke? Hercules? *You* broke it. You broke the ancient law and order of the world: that the living are the living and the dead are the dead.

APOLLO:

Yes—one small ray of light fell where light had never fallen before.

DEATH:

You broke that law, and now you're caught up in its consequences. You're losing your happiness and your very wits because you can't make yourself known to them. And you're behaving like the rejected lover who dashes into the beloved's house and kills everyone there.

APOLLO:

I *have* made myself known to them. I have set my story in motion.

DEATH:

Your lesson.

APOLLO:

Yes, my lesson—that I can bring back from the dead only those who have offered their lives for others.

DEATH:

You brought back *one,* and now you are hurling thousands and thousands into my kingdom.

APOLLO:

Yes, I must bring ruin and havoc, for only so will they remember the story. In the stories that are longest remembered, death plays a large role.

DEATH:

    Shuddering.

This light! This light! All these plague-stricken do not interest me. There is one mortal here that I am waiting for . . . she who escaped me once.

APOLLO:

Alcestis? You will never have her.

DEATH:

She is mortal!

APOLLO:

Yes.

DEATH:
She is *mortal!*

APOLLO:
All mortal. Nothing but mortal.

DEATH:
What are you going to do? You cannot steal her a second time?

APOLLO:
Death, the sun is risen. You are shaking.

DEATH:
Yes, but give me an answer. I am in a hurry.

APOLLO:
Start accustoming yourself to a change.

DEATH:
I?

APOLLO:
One ray of light has already reached your kingdom.

DEATH:
> *In headlong flight to his cave, shrieking.*

There'll be no more. No second one. No more light. No more.
No change!

> *Exit. The light fades from* APOLLO, *who disappears.*
> *Enter from the road—through the palace gate, left open—*EPI-
> MENES, *21, and* CHERIANDER, *also 21. They are holding their
> cloaks about their noses. Under their cloaks they wear short
> swords.* CHERIANDER *comes forward eagerly and looks about
> him with awe.* EPIMENES *follows him, morose and bitter.*

CHERIANDER:
The palace of Admetus and Alcestis! . . . And was Apollo here?

Where did He place His feet—here, or here?

> EPIMENES *nods, scarcely raising his eyes from the ground.*

And Hercules brought your mother back from the dead . . . where?

> EPIMENES *indicates the cave.* CHERIANDER *goes quickly down to it.*

That I have lived to see this place! Look, Epimenes! There is your old friend Pytho guarding the door. Speak to him so that we can drink at the spring. This water, at least, is not poisoned.

EPIMENES:

You remember me, Pytho? He scarcely stirs.

CHERIANDER:

Make the offering, and let us drink.

EPIMENES:

"Sources of life—earth, air . . ." No, Cheriander, I cannot. How can I say the prayer we said here so many hundred times? In the morning my father and mother would bring us here. How could all this have happened? The God turned his face away. My father killed. My brother and sister killed. Myself sent away by night to live among strangers. My mother a slave—or dead. And the land under pestilence and the dead bodies lying unburied under the sun. To whom do I make a prayer?

CHERIANDER:

> *With quiet resolution.*

We are leaving Pherai. We are going out of that gate now. You are not ready to do what we came to do, and I will not help you.

EPIMENES:

I can do what I have to do without prayer or offering. Justice and revenge speak for themselves. To strike! To strike into his throat. Yes, and to strike his daughter, Laodamia, too.

CHERIANDER:

Epimenes, I will not help you. This is not the way we planned it. Kill or be killed, as you wish. I have not crossed Greece with you to take part in a mere butchery.

EPIMENES:

You want me to make a prayer? To whom? To Apollo, who has blasted this house with His hatred?

CHERIANDER:

He descends, and putting his hands on EPIMENES'S *shoulders, shakes him in solemn anger.*

Are you the first man to have suffered? Cruelty, injustice, murder, and humiliation—is it only here that those things can be found? Have you forgotten that we came here to establish justice? That you yourself said that men of themselves could never have arrived at justice—that it was planted in their minds by the gods?

They gaze sternly at one another.

EPIMENES:

Quietly, looking down.

I do not deserve to have such a friend.

Enter ALCESTIS, *left, carrying the water jar on her shoulder.*

CHERIANDER:

Are you ready to make the offering?

EPIMENES *recites the ritual, solemnly, but all but inaudibly.*
They both drink. CHERIANDER *starts up the path, vigorously.*

I am ready to knock at the palace doors.

He sees ALCESTIS. *He hurries back to the spring, and says to* EPIMENES:

There is an old woman here. We will see what we can learn from her.

Alcestis has taken a few steps down the path, but seeing the men, draws back. Cheriander comes up the path to her.

Old woman, is this the palace of Agis, King of Thessaly?

Her eyes go at once to the gate. Cheriander returns to Epimenes.

She seems to be a slave. Perhaps it is your mother.

EPIMENES:

Goes quickly up the path, looks closely at Alcestis, then says brusquely:

No.

CHERIANDER:
You are sure?

EPIMENES:
Shortly.
Sure. Certain.

CHERIANDER:

Tell me, old woman, has this pestilence taken lives in the palace?
She shakes her head.
King Agis lives here with his family—with a young daughter, Laodamia?
She nods.
Tell me: the guards he has about him—did he bring them from Thrace, or are they of this country?
No answer.

EPIMENES:

Perhaps she is deaf, or dumb.
Louder.
Does he often make journeys back to his own country—to Thrace?

ALCESTIS:

You are in danger here. You must go—you must go at once.

EPIMENES:

Oh, she can speak. Tell me, old mother, were you here in the days of King Admetus and Queen Alcestis?

ALCESTIS:

Who are you? From where have you come?

EPIMENES:

Did you know them? Had you talked with them?
>   *She nods.*

King Admetus is dead?
>   *She nods.*

Is Queen Alcestis alive?
>   *No sign.*

Here in the palace?
>   *Her eyes return again to the gate. He adds impatiently:*

By the immortal gods, since you can speak, speak!

ALCESTIS:

You must go at once. But tell me . . . tell me: who are you?

CHERIANDER:

>   *Staring at* ALCESTIS, *but urgently striking* EPIMENES's *forearm.*

Look again. Look closely. Are you sure?

EPIMENES:

Sure! These mountain women are all the same. They all have this silence, this slyness.

ALCESTIS:

How did you come in at that gate? King Agis will certainly have you killed.

CHERIANDER:

No. We bring a message to King Agis that he will be glad to hear.

ALCESTIS:

Repeatedly shaking her head.
There is no message now that will save your lives, young man.
Go. Take the road to the north and go quickly.

EPIMENES:

The message we bring will make us very welcome. We have come
to tell him of the death of an enemy—of his greatest enemy.

CHERIANDER:

There is no need to tell it now.

EPIMENES:

Whom he lives in dread of.
Shaking her head, ALCESTIS *passes him and starts down the path.*
We come to tell him of the death of Epimenes, the son of King
Admetus and Queen Alcestis. He will be glad enough to hear of
that.
*ALCESTIS is near the spring. She stops, lifts her head, and puts
her hand to her heart, letting her jar slip.*

CHERIANDER:

Going to her and taking her jar.
Let me carry your jar, old woman.

ALCESTIS:

Suddenly.
You are Epimenes!

CHERIANDER:

Short laugh.
No, old woman. Epimenes is dead.

ALCESTIS:
You have proof of this?

CHERIANDER:
Yes, proof.
> *He has filled the jar and is starting up the path.*

ALCESTIS:
We have always thought that he would return . . . in secret, or disguise. My eyes are failing.
> *Eagerly.*

You are Epimenes!

CHERIANDER:
No, mother, no.

ALCESTIS:
You knew him—you talked with him?

CHERIANDER:
Yes, many times. Where can I carry this for you?

ALCESTIS:
> *At the top of the path, peers into* EPIMENES's *face.*

Let me look at you.
> *Then gazing into* CHERIANDER's *face.*

Do not tell lies to an old woman. He sent no message?

EPIMENES:
None.

ALCESTIS:
None?

EPIMENES:
None but this. Can you see this belt? Queen Alcestis wove this for King Admetus before Epimenes was born.

ALCESTIS:

Peers at it, and gives a cry.

What manner of young man was he who gave you this belt?

EPIMENES:

Mastering his impatience; as to a deaf person.

Old woman, is Queen Alcestis near? Make some answer: yes or
no. This is unendurable. Can you call Queen Alcestis, or can't
you?

ALCESTIS:

I am Alcestis.

CHERIANDER:

After amazed silence, falls on one knee; gazing into her face.

You . . . you are Alcestis?

EPIMENES:

Standing rigid, one fist on his forehead.

I am ashamed to say my name.

He also sinks to one knee.

I am Epimenes.

ALCESTIS:

Yes—yes.

Her eyes turning from palace to road.

But in this danger . . . this danger . . .

EPIMENES:

Forgive . . . me.

ALCESTIS:

Touching his head.

You are an impatient, self-willed young man, as I was an impatient, self-willed girl. It is time you were more like your father.

EPIMENES:
You unhappy—

ALCESTIS:
> *Almost sharply.*

No. No, Epimenes. Do not call me unhappy.

EPIMENES:
This misery . . .

ALCESTIS:
No! Learn to know unhappiness when you see it. There is only one misery, and that is ignorance—ignorance of what our lives are. That is misery and despair.

CHERIANDER:
> *Rising, intent.*

Ignorance?

ALCESTIS:
Great happiness was given to me once, yes . . . but shall I forget that now? And forget the one who gave it to me? All that has happened since came from the same hands that gave me the happiness. I shall not doubt that it is good and has a part in something I cannot see. . . . You must go now.

EPIMENES:
> *Rising.*

We have come to kill King Agis and to regain the throne.
> ALCESTIS *starts turning her face from side to side and murmuring, "No. No."*

Our plans have been made in detail. This very night—

ALCESTIS:
No. No, Epimenes. The plague, the pestilence, has taken the place of all that. King Agis has only one thought, and one fear

—not for himself, but for his child, Laodamia. The God is bringing things to pass in His own way.

CHERIANDER:
We will do what she says, Epimenes, and go now.

ALCESTIS:
Come back . . . in ten days. Go north. Hold your cloaks before your faces and go north.

CHERIANDER:
Get your cloak, Epimenes.
> EPIMENES *descends to the spring.*

ALCESTIS:
Where is your home, young man?

CHERIANDER:
In Euboea—under Mount Dirphys.

ALCESTIS:
Is your mother living?

CHERIANDER:
Yes, Queen Alcestis.

ALCESTIS:
Does she know my name?

CHERIANDER:
Every child in Greece knows your name!

ALCESTIS:
Tell her . . . Alcestis thanks her.
> EPIMENES *is beside her; she touches him lightly.*
Remember—I have not been unhappy. I was once miserable and in despair: I was saved from that.

Pointing.

Go through that grove . . . and follow the river.

> *Sounds of* TOWNSPEOPLE *approaching. More breaking of gates.*
> *They come on to the edge of the stage, shouting. The* WATCHMAN
> *and* GUARDS *come out of the palace in alarm.* ALCESTIS *beckons*
> *to the young men to descend and hide themselves by the spring.*
> *The* GUARDS *keep the people back by holding their spears hori-*
> *zontally before them.*

TOWNSPEOPLE:

Water! We want water from the palace spring! The water's been
poisoned. King Agis, help us!

GUARDS:

Back! Back and out—all of you!

> *Enter from the palace* KING AGIS. *He is dressed in a barbaric,*
> *ornate costume. He is 40; a thick cap of black hair over a low*
> *forehead. His face is also streaked with ashes.*

AGIS:

How did these people get into the court?

TOWNSPEOPLE:

King Agis, help us!

AGIS:

This eternal "Help us!" I'm doing what I can. Which one of you
let these people in?

GUARDS:

> *In confusion.*

Sire—they've broken the gates. We can't hold them.

AGIS:

Cowards! Do your duty. You're afraid to go near them, that's the
trouble.

To the TOWNSPEOPLE.

Stand back!

To a GUARD.

What is that they were saying about water?

FIRST GUARD:

They say, Your Greatness, they think that the springs in the town have been poisoned, and they want some water from the springs in the palace.

AGIS:

Very well, you shall have water from these springs.

> *Holding a corner of his robe before his nose, he points to a man who has crawled far forward on his knees.*

Get back, you! People of Pherai, I have news for you. I thought I had done all a king could do; and now I find there is one more thing to be done. Where's this Alcestis?

WATCHMAN:

She is here, Your Greatness.

AGIS:

> *Turns and looks at her in long, slow contempt, and says slowly:*

So . . . you . . . are . . . the bringer of all this evil! This is a great day, people of Pherai, for at last we have come to the heart of this matter. If it can be shown that this woman has brought this disease upon us, she will be stoned to death or driven from the country.

To ALCESTIS.

Woman, is it true that you were dead—dead and buried—and that you were brought back to life?

ALCESTIS:

It is true.

AGIS:

And that you and your husband believed that this was done by Hercules, with the aid of Apollo, and as a sign of Apollo's favor?

ALCESTIS:

We believed it, and it is true.

AGIS:

And is it true that you and your husband believed that Apollo was here for a year's time, out of love and favor for you and Thessaly?

ALCESTIS:

We believed it, and it is true.

AGIS:

And where is that love now? People of Pherai, this is Apollo's land. If Apollo formerly extended favor to this woman and to her family, is it not clear to you now that His favor has turned to hatred?

The crowd is silent.

Yes or no?

Contradictory murmurs.

What? You are of mixed mind? You dolts! Have you forgotten that this plague is raging among you? Watchman!

WATCHMAN:

Yes, sire?

AGIS:

Before the gates of the palace were closed, did you see the effects of the disease, and how it struck?

WATCHMAN:

Yes, sire, I saw it.

AGIS:

Describe it!

WATCHMAN:

Your Greatness, it is not just one—there are three diseases. The first comes suddenly, like—
> *A* GUARD *has come from the palace, and presents himself before* KING AGIS.

AGIS:
> *Irritably.*

Well, what is it? What is it?

SECOND GUARD:

Sire, your daughter is beating on her door. She says she wishes to be let out. She says she wishes to be where you are. Without stopping she is beating on her door.

AGIS:
> *With a reflection of his tenderness for her; urgently.*

Tell her that I shall be with her soon; that I have work to do here. Tell her to be patient; tell her that I shall come to her soon.

SECOND GUARD:

Yes, sire.
> *He starts toward the palace door.*

AGIS:

Wait!
> *Torn.*

Tell her to be patient. I shall take her from her room for a walk in the garden later.

SECOND GUARD:

Yes, sire.
> *Exit.*

AGIS:

> *To the* WATCHMAN.

Three? Three diseases, you say?

WATCHMAN:

The first one strikes suddenly, Your Greatness, like lightning.

AGIS:

> *With a shudder; turning to* ALCESTIS.

Your work, old woman!

ALCESTIS:

No! No!

WATCHMAN:

> *His hands on his stomach.*

Like fire. That's the one that strikes young people and children.

AGIS:

> *Beside himself.*

Children! Idiot! Don't you know better than to say words of ill omen here? I'll have your tongue torn out. Avert, you immortal gods, avert the omen! Hear not the omen!

> *To the* WATCHMAN.

I want no more of this.

> *Turning to the palace in despairing frustration.*

Oh, go away—all of you! Who shall save us from this night . . . this swamp . . . this evil cloud?

> *He turns his head from side to side in helplessness and revulsion; then suddenly pulls himself together; resolutely, pointing at* ALCESTIS.

Speak then! Apollo the God hates you, and through you has brought this curse upon Thessaly.

> ALCESTIS, *in silence, looks at him with a level gaze.*

Is that not so? Speak!

ALCESTIS:

> *Taking her time.*

When Apollo came to this city, King Agis, his priest Teiresias said that that great honor brought with it a great peril.

AGIS:

Peril?

ALCESTIS:

You stand in that peril now. This floor is still warm—is hot— from the footprints of the God. . . .

> *As though to herself, almost dreamily.*

For a long time I did not understand this. It is solitude—and slavery—that have made it clear to me. Beware what you do here, King Agis.

AGIS:

> *Throws up his chin, curtly dismissing this warning.*

Answer my question.

ALCESTIS:

The gods are not like you and me, King Agis—but at times we are like them. They do not love us for a day or a year and then hate what they have loved. Nor do you love your child Laodamia today and tomorrow drive her out upon the road.

AGIS:

> *Outraged.*

Do not name her, you . . . you bringer of death and destruction!

> *He starts toward the palace door.*

ALCESTIS:

We ask of them health . . . and riches . . . and our happiness. But they are trying to give us something else, and better: understanding. And we are so quick to refuse their gift. . . . No! No! Apollo has not turned His face away from me. . . . People of Pherai, had you ever been told that King Admetus was unjust to you?

TOWNSPEOPLE:
No, Queen Alcestis.

ALCESTIS:
Or I?

TOWNSPEOPLE:
No-o-o-o, Queen Alcestis!

ALCESTIS:
Do you believe that this disease has been sent to punish you for any wickedness of ours?

TOWNSPEOPLE:
No! No!

ALCESTIS:
If Hercules brought someone back from the dead, do you think he could have done it without the full approval of the gods?

TOWNSPEOPLE:
No! No!

AGIS:
Then what is the cause of this pestilence?

ALCESTIS:
It has been sent . . . to call our attention to . . . to make us stop, to open our eyes . . .

AGIS:
To call our attention to what, Alcestis?

ALCESTIS:

Lifted head, as though listening.

I don't know. To some sign.

There is a moment of suspended waiting. Then suddenly the
FIRST GUARD, *at the head of the path, sees the two* YOUNG MEN
and cries:

FIRST GUARD:

Sire, there are two strangers here.

AGIS:

Coming forward as near as he dares.

How did they come here? Guards! Close in on them!

GUARDS *gather above and in front of them.*

Throw down your swords!

EPIMENES:

Never, King Agis!

AGIS:

What can you do—caught in that hole there? Throw down your
swords!

ALCESTIS *has been shaking her head from side to side, and*
murmuring, "King Agis, King Agis . . ."

To ALCESTIS.

You brought them in. Neither you nor they have put ashes on
your faces.

To the GUARDS.

Kill them! Kill them!

Two GUARDS *start gingerly down the path.*

Cowards! Traitors! Do what I command!

Suddenly a THIRD GUARD *on the stage is stricken with the*
plague. He throws down his spear and cries:

THIRD GUARD:

King Agis! Water! The plague! I'm on fire. Save me! Help me! I'm on fire!

> *Intermittently he yawns.*

AGIS:

> *Recoiling, as all recoil.*

Drive him out! Strike his back with your spears.

THIRD GUARD:

> *Alternately lurching from side to side, and yawning, and crying out.*

Water! Water! Sleeeeep!

AGIS:

> *Holding his hands before his face.*

Push him out into the road.

> *General tumult. The* THIRD GUARD *tries to drag himself to the gate. Other* GUARDS *and* TOWNSPEOPLE, *averting their faces, try, with spears, with kicks, to hurry his departure. In these horrors, the* GUARDS *have removed their attention from* EPI-MENES *and* CHERIANDER. *For a second all that can be heard is exhausted panting.*

AGIS:

> *Screaming.*

My wagons! My horses! . . . To Thrace! To Thrace!

> *To* ALCESTIS.

Take back your Thessaly the Hospitable, Queen Alcestis! Rule over your dead and dying. . . .

EPIMENES:

Now, Cheriander!

> *They rush upon the stage.*

CHERIANDER:

Strike, Epimenes!

EPIMENES:

Agis—I am Epimenes, son of King Admetus!

AGIS:

Who? What is this? Guards!
> ALCESTIS, *shaking her head, stands in front of* KING AGIS, *and with raised hands opposes* EPIMENES.

ALCESTIS:

No, Epimenes! No!

EPIMENES:

> *Outraged by* ALCESTIS's *attitude.*
Mother! The moment has come. He killed my father!

ALCESTIS:

Don't do it!

AGIS:

Guards!
> *Taking distraught steps, right and left.*
Coward! Guards!

CHERIANDER:

Listen to your mother, Epimenes.

ALCESTIS:

> *Her back to* AGIS, *but talking to him.*
Yes, King Agis, go back to your own kingdom.

AGIS:

Is that your son? Alcestis, answer me: is this your son?
> *In rage and frustration at seeing his revenge frustrated,* EP-

IMENES *is on one knee, beating the floor with the hilt of his own sword.*

EPIMENES:

Revenge! Revenge!

ALCESTIS:

Epimenes, remember your father's words: that the murderer cuts the sinews of his own heart.

EPIMENES:

Sobbing, his forehead near the ground.

He killed my father . . . my brother . . . my sister . . .

The SECOND GUARD *rushes from the palace.*

SECOND GUARD:

King Agis! Your daughter, the Princess Laodamia! She is beating on her door and calling for you—in pain, King Agis, in pain!

AGIS:

Arms upraised.

The gods avert! Laodamia! Laodamia! Avert, you immortal gods!

AGIS *rushes into the palace.*

ALCESTIS:

Standing over EPIMENES *and placing her hand on his shoulder.*

A man who has known the joys of revenge may never know any other joy. That is the voice of your father.

She turns to the TOWNSPEOPLE *and says calmly and impartially:*

Friends, go to your homes and get baskets and jars. Go to the quarries beyond the South Gate, where sulfur is. Epimenes, you remember the quarries where you played as a child? That yellow sulfur that the workers in iron used . . . Burn it in the streets. Spread it on the dead.

To the GUARDS.

Help them in this work; there is nothing more for you to do here.
Epimenes, stand—stand up. Direct them in this.

EPIMENES:

Getting up.

Yes, Mother.

With quiet authority; to GUARDS *and* TOWNSPEOPLE.

Come with me.

They start off, but CHERIANDER *returns and adds softly, in awe:*

CHERIANDER:

Queen Alcestis . . . the sign you spoke of—from Apollo the God.
Was this decision of King Agis—was that the sign?

ALCESTIS:

With lifted listening head.

No . . . the sign has not come yet.

CHERIANDER:

With youthful ardor.

You are the sign! You are message and sign, Queen Alcestis!

ALCESTIS:

Almost insensible, shaking her head; softly.

No . . . no . . .

CHERIANDER dashes out after EPIMENES. *Enter from the palace*
KING AGIS, *howling with grief.*

AGIS:

She is dead! Laodamia is dead! Twelve years old. She is dead. . . .

*He beats his fists against columns and walls. He stamps down
the stairs, then up them again.*

Twelve years old. Her arms around my neck. In excruciating
pain. "Father, help me . . . Father, help me!" . . . Her hair. Her
mother's face. Her eyes, her eyes.

He sees ALCESTIS.

You—you brought this! You did this!

ALCESTIS:

Murmuring through his words, as if entreating.

Agis . . . Agis . . . Agis . . .

AGIS:

Seizing her hand and touching it to his forehead and chest.

Give me this plague. Let it destroy us all. "Father, help me!" She was everything to me. And she is dead—dead—dead!

ALCESTIS:

Agis . . . Agis . . .

AGIS:

You—whom Hercules brought back from the dead—you could do this.

An idea strikes him.

Hercules brought you back. Where was it? Was it here?

He stumbles down the path.

There?

He ascends the path quickly.

Tell me, Alcestis—how did Hercules do it? What happened below there?

ALCESTIS *shakes her head silently.*

Show me what he did and I shall do it. Laodamia, I shall come for you. Answer me, Alcestis!

ALCESTIS:

Agis, I saw nothing. I heard nothing.

AGIS:

You are lying.

ALCESTIS:

Agis, listen to me—I have something to say to you.

AGIS:

Speak! Speak!

ALCESTIS:

"Father, help me!"

AGIS:

Do not mock me.

ALCESTIS:

I am not mocking you. What was Laodamia saying, King Agis?

AGIS:

She was in pain, pain, excruciating pain!

ALCESTIS:

Yes, but that was not all. What more did she mean?

AGIS:

What more?

ALCESTIS:

The bitterness of death, King Agis, is part pain—but that is not all. The last bitterness of death is not parting—though that is great grief. I died . . . once. What is the last bitterness of death, King Agis?

AGIS:

Tell me!

ALCESTIS:

It is the despair that one has not lived. It is the despair that one's life has been without meaning. That it has been nonsense; happy or unhappy, that it has been senseless. "Father, help me."

AGIS:

She loved me, Alcestis.

ALCESTIS:

Yes.

AGIS:

She *loved* me.

ALCESTIS:

Yes, but love is not enough.

AGIS:

It *was*. It was for her and it was for me. I will not listen to you.

ALCESTIS:

Love is not the meaning. It is one of the signs that there is a meaning—it is only one of the signs that there is a meaning. Laodamia is in despair and asks that you help her. That is what death is—it is despair. Her life is vain and empty, until you give it a meaning.

AGIS:

What meaning could I give it?

ALCESTIS:

> *Quietly.*

You are a brutal, cruel, and ignorant man.

> *Brief silence.*

You killed *my* Laodamia. Three times. Senselessly. Even you do not know how many times you have killed Laodamia.

AGIS:

No!

102

ALCESTIS:

You don't know. Go back to your kingdom. There, and only there, can you help Laodamia.

> AGIS *comes up the path and, passing her, goes toward the palace door.*

All the dead, King Agis . . .

> *She points to the entrance to the underworld.*

all those millions lie imploring us to show them that their lives were not empty and foolish.

AGIS:

And what is this meaning that I can give to Laodamia's life?

ALCESTIS:

Today you have begun to understand that.

AGIS:

> *His head against the post of the palace door.*

No.

ALCESTIS:

I was taught these things. Even I. You will learn them, King Agis. . . . Through Laodamia's suffering you will learn them.

> *Broken, he goes through the palace door.*
>
> *During his slow exit, the light begins to fall on* APOLLO, *entering from the palace doors. In this descent, He wears His cloak, but the hood has fallen back on His shoulders, showing a garland around His head. He first addresses* ALCESTIS *from the doors; then moves behind her.*
>
> *Left alone,* ALCESTIS *closes her eyes and takes a few steps left. Her head seems to bend with great weariness; she seems to shrink to a great age. She turns right and starts to move toward the gate to the road, her eyes half open.*

103

APOLLO:

A few more steps, Alcestis. Through the gate . . . and across the road . . . and into my grove.

ALCESTIS:

So far . . . and so high . . .

APOLLO:

Now another step. It is not a hill. You do not have to raise your foot.

ALCESTIS:

It is too far. Let me find my grave here.

APOLLO:

You will not have that grave, Alcestis.

ALCESTIS:

Oh, yes. I want my grave. . . .

APOLLO:

The grave means an end. You will not have that ending. You are the first of a great number that will not have that ending. Still another step, Alcestis.

ALCESTIS:

And will there be grandchildren, and the grandchildren of grandchildren . . .?

APOLLO:

Beyond all counting.

ALCESTIS:

Yes . . . What was his name?

APOLLO:

Admetus.

ALCESTIS:
Yes. And the shining one I wanted to serve?

APOLLO:
Apollo.

ALCESTIS:
Yes . . .
> *Near the gate.*
All the thousands of days . . . and the world of cares . . .
> *Raising her head, with closed eyes.*
And whom do I thank for all the happiness?

APOLLO:
Friends do not ask one another that question.
> *She goes out.*
> APOLLO *raises His voice, as though to ensure that she will hear Him beyond the wall.*
Those who have loved one another do not ask one another that question . . . Alcestis.

CURTAIN

Transition from
THE ALCESTIAD
to
THE DRUNKEN SISTERS

At the close of the three acts of The Alcestiad a curtain falls.
APOLLO *comes before the curtain.*

APOLLO:
> *To the audience.*

Wait! Wait! We have still one more thing to do. We are in Greece, and here we do not believe that audiences should return to their homes immediately after watching stories that present what is difficult and painful in human life. Here we have this custom: we require that the poet write a short satyr play in the spirit of diversion—even of the comical.

> *Confidentially.*

We claim that the tragic insight cannot stand alone. It tends to its own excess. As one of you

> *Pointing into the audience.*

has said: Neither Death nor the Sun permits itself to be gazed at fixedly. And further, we require that this satyr play deal with some element—some secondary aspect—of the preceding play. So—what shall we show you? Teiresias—the six-hundred-year-old, the too-much-loved? How from time to time the gods made him young again; how from time to time they even changed him into a woman? And the quarrel between Zeus and Hera about that?

He starts laughing but tries to control himself.

No, no—that's not suitable here. That play is too coarse. The Greeks have stomachs strong enough to endure such unseemly matters, but

He is again overcome with laughter.

it is . . . No, no—not here. Or shall we show you the story about the sisters of Queen Alcestis? Her father, King Pelias, was an old fool and her two sisters were not very clever. That often happens in families—there is just one intelligent person. We could show you how the archcook Medea whispered into the sisters' ears, pretending to show them how they could make their dear father young again. . . .

Suddenly changing his tone.

No! It is true that there are people who laugh only when they hear about something cruel. That play is a heap of cruelties, and when you went home you would be ashamed of yourselves for having been amused by it.

We have another: it is not very funny. Tonight did you ask yourselves how it was possible that the life of King Admetus was extended? Those great ladies the weird sisters, the Fates—can they be bribed? We shall show you how it happened.

He starts taking off his outer robes, under which he is dressed as a kitchen boy, and calls into the wings: "My hat! My hat!"

In this little play I am again Apollo, in the disguise of a kitchen boy.

From the wings are reached out to him a large cone-shaped straw hat and a belt, from which the effects of a kitchen boy—onions, etc.—hang. He calls into the wings: "My bottles!," sets his hat on his head, and puts on the belt.

I hate disguises, I hate drunkenness—

From the wings he receives a rope, from which three bottles hang.

but see these bottles I have hanging around my neck? I hate lies and stratagems—but I've come to do crookedly what even All-

Father Zeus could not do without guile: extend a human life.

Calling through the curtain to the rear or into the wings: "All ready?" and then turning again to the audience.

Yes, all is ready for the satyr play, to conclude the solemn trilogy of *The Alcestiad.*

He remains standing at the proscenium pillar as the curtain rises.

THE

DRUNKEN SISTERS

The three FATES *are seated on a bench largely hidden by their voluminous draperies. They wear the masks of old women, touched by the grotesque but with vestiges of nobility. Seated are* CLOTHO *with her spindle,* LACHESIS *with the bulk of the thread of life on her lap, and* ATROPOS *with her scissors. They rock back and forth as they work, passing the threads from right to left. The audience watches them for a time in silence, broken only by a faint humming from* CLOTHO.

CLOTHO:
What is it that goes first on four legs, then on two legs? Don't tell me! Don't tell me!

LACHESIS:
>*Bored.*
You know it!

CLOTHO:
Let me pretend that I don't know it.

ATROPOS:
There are no new riddles. We know them all.

LACHESIS:
How boring our life is without riddles! Clotho, make up a riddle.

CLOTHO:

Be quiet, then, and give me a moment to think. . . . What is it that
. . . What is it that . . .?

> *Enter* APOLLO, *disguised.*

APOLLO:

> *To the audience.*

These are the great sisters—the Fates. Clotho weaves the threads
of life; Lachesis measures the length of each; Atropos cuts them
short. In their monotonous work of deciding our lives they are
terribly bored, and like so many people who are bored, they find
great pleasure in games—in enigmas and riddles. Naturally they
can't play cards, because their hands are always busy with the
threads of life.

ATROPOS:

Sister! Your elbow! Do your work without striking me.

LACHESIS:

I can't help it—this thread is s-o-o l-o-o-ong! Never have I had to
reach so far.

CLOTHO:

Long and gray and dirty! All those years a slave!

LACHESIS:

So it is!

> *To* ATROPOS.

Cut it, dear sister.

> ATROPOS *cuts it—click!*

And now this one; cut this. It's a blue one—blue for bravery: blue
and short.

ATROPOS:

So easy to see!

> *Click.*

THE DRUNKEN SISTERS

LACHESIS:
You almost cut that purple one, Atropos.

ATROPOS:
This one? Purple for a king?

LACHESIS:
Yes; watch what you're doing, dear. It's the life of Admetus, King of Thessaly.

APOLLO:
Aside.
Aie!

LACHESIS:
I've marked it clearly. He's to die at sunset.

APOLLO:
To the audience.
No! No!

LACHESIS:
He's the favorite of Apollo, as was his father before him, and all that tiresome house of Thessaly. The queen Alcestis will be a widow tonight.

APOLLO:
To the audience.
Alcestis! Alcestis! No!

LACHESIS:
There'll be howling in Thessaly. There'll be rolling on the ground and tearing of garments. . . . Not now, dear; there's an hour yet.

THE DRUNKEN SISTERS

APOLLO:

> *Aside.*

To work! To work, Apollo the Crooked!

> *He starts the motions of running furiously while remaining in one place, but stops suddenly and addresses the audience.*

Is there anyone here who does not know that old story—the reason why King Admetus and his queen Alcestis are dear to me?

> *He sits on the ground and continues talking with raised forefinger.*

Was it ten years ago? I am little concerned with time. I am the god of the sun; it is always light where I am. Perhaps ten years ago. My father and the father of us all was filled up with anger against me. What had I done?

> *He moves his finger back and forth.*

Do not ask that now; let it be forgotten. . . . He laid upon me a punishment. He ordered that I should descend to earth and live for a year among men—I, as a man among men, as a servant. Half hidden, known and not known, I chose to be a herdsman of King Admetus of Thessaly. I lived the life of a man, as close to them as I am to you now, as close to the just and to the unjust. Each day the King gave orders to the other herdsmen and myself; each day the Queen gave thought to what went well or ill with us and our families. I came to love King Admetus and Queen Alcestis and through them I came to love all men. And now Admetus must die.

> *Rising.*

No! I have laid my plans. I shall prevent it. To work. To work, Apollo the Crooked.

> *He again starts the motions of running furiously while remaining in one place. He complains noisily:*

Oh, my back! Aie, aie. They beat me, but worst of all they've made me late. I'll be beaten again.

116

LACHESIS:

Who's the sniveler?

APOLLO:

Don't stop me now. I haven't a moment to talk. I'm late already. Besides, my errand's a terrible secret. I can't say a word.

ATROPOS:

Throw your yarn around him, Lachesis. What's the fool doing with a secret? It's we who have all the secrets.

> *The threads in the laps of the* SISTERS *are invisible to the audience.* LACHESIS *now rises and swings her hands three times in wide circles above her head as though she were about to fling a lasso, then hurls the noose across the stage.* APOLLO *makes the gesture of being caught. With each strong pull by* LACHESIS, APOLLO *is dragged nearer to her. During the following speeches* LACHESIS *lifts her end of the strands high in the air, alternately pulling* APOLLO *up, almost strangling him, and flinging him again to the ground.*

APOLLO:

Ladies, beautiful ladies, let me go. If I'm late all Olympus will be in an uproar. Aphrodite will be mad with fear—but oh, already I've said too much. My orders were to come immediately, and to say nothing—especially not to women. The thing's of no interest to men. Dear ladies, let me go.

ATROPOS:

Pull on your yarn, sister.

APOLLO:

You're choking me. You're squeezing me to death.

LACHESIS:

> *Forcefully.*

Stop your whining and tell your secret at once.

APOLLO:

I can't. I dare not.

ATROPOS:

Pull harder, sister. Boy, speak or strangle.

> *She makes the gesture of choking him.*

APOLLO:

Ow! Ow!—Wait! I'll tell the half of it, if you let me go.

ATROPOS:

Tell the whole or we'll hang you up in the air in that noose.

APOLLO:

I'll tell, I'll tell. But—

> *He looks about him fearfully.*

promise me! Swear by the Styx that you'll not tell anyone, and swear by Lethe that you'll forget it.

LACHESIS:

We have only one oath—by Acheron. And we never swear it—least of all to a sniveling slave. Tell us what you know, or you'll be by all three rivers in a minute.

APOLLO:

I tremble at what I am about to say. I . . . ssh . . . I carry . . . here . . . in these bottles . . . Oh, ladies, let me go. Let me go.

CLOTHO and ATROPOS:

Pull, sister.

APOLLO:

No! No! I'll tell you. I am carrying the wine for ... for Aphrodite. Once every ten days she renews her beauty ... by ... drinking this.

ATROPOS:

Liar! Fool! She has nectar and ambrosia, as they all have.

APOLLO:

Confidentially.
But is she not the fairest? ... It is the love gift of Hephaistos; from the vineyards of Dionysos; from grapes ripened under the eye of Apollo—of Apollo who tells no lies.
The SISTERS *confidentially to one another in blissful anticipation.*

LACHESIS and ATROPOS and CLOTHO:

Sisters!

ATROPOS:

Like sugar.
Pass the bottles up, dear boy.

APOLLO:

In terror.
Not that! Ladies! It is enough that I have told you the secret! Not that!

ATROPOS:

Surely, Lachesis, you can find on your lap the thread of this worthless slave—a yellow one destined for a long life?

APOLLO:

Falling on his knees.
Spare me!

ATROPOS:

> *To* LACHESIS.

Look, that's it—the sallow one, with the tangle in it of dishonesty, and the stiffness of obstinacy, and the ravel-ravel of stupidity. Pass it over to me, dear.

APOLLO:

> *His forehead touching the floor.*

Oh, that I had never been born!

LACHESIS:

> *To* ATROPOS.

This is it.

> *With a sigh.*

I'd planned to give him five score.

APOLLO:

> *Rising and extending the bottles, sobbing.*

Here, take them! Take them! I'll be killed anyway. Aphrodite will kill me. My life's over.

ATROPOS:

> *Strongly, as the* SISTERS *take the bottles.*

Not one more word out of you. Put your hand on your mouth. We're tired of listening to you.

> APOLLO, *released of the noose, flings himself face down upon the ground, his shoulders heaving. The* SISTERS *put the flagons to their lips. They drink and moan with pleasure.*

LACHESIS and ATROPOS and CLOTHO:
Sisters!

LACHESIS:
Sister, how do I look?

ATROPOS:
Oh, I could eat you. And I?

CLOTHO:
Sister, how do I look?

LACHESIS:
Beautiful! Beautiful! And I?

ATROPOS:
And not a mirror on all the mountain, or a bit of still water, to tell us which of us is the fairest.

LACHESIS:
Dreamily, passing her hand over her face.
I feel like . . . I feel as I did when Kronos followed me about, trying to catch me in a dark corner.

ATROPOS:
Poseidon was beside himself—dashing across the plains trying to engulf me.

CLOTHO:
My own father—who can blame him?—began to forget himself.

ATROPOS:
Whispering.
This is not such a worthless fellow, after all. And he's not bad-looking.
To CLOTHO.
Ask him what he sees.

LACHESIS:
Ask him which of us is the fairest.

CLOTHO:
Boy! Boy! You bay meek. I mean, you . . . you may thpeak. Thpeak to him, Lakethith; I've lotht my tongue.

121

LACHESIS:

Boy, look at us well! You may tell us which is the fairest.

> APOLLO *has remained face downward on the ground. He now rises and gazes at the* SISTERS. *He acts as if blinded: he cowers and uncovers his eyes, gazing first at one and then at another.*

APOLLO:

What have I done? This splendor! What have I done? You—and you—and you! Kill me if you will, but I cannot say which one is the fairest.

> *Falling on his knees.*

Oh, ladies—if so much beauty has not made you cruel, let me now go and hide myself. Aphrodite will hear of this. Let me escape to Crete and take up my old work.

ATROPOS:

What was your former work, dear boy?

APOLLO:

I helped my father in the marketplace; I was a teller of stories and riddles.

> *The* SISTERS *are transfixed. Then almost with a scream.*

SISTERS:

What's that? What's that you said?

APOLLO:

A teller of stories and riddles. Do the beautiful ladies enjoy riddles?

SISTERS:

> *Rocking from side to side and slapping one another.*

Sisters, do we enjoy riddles?

THE DRUNKEN SISTERS

ATROPOS:

Oh, he would only know the old ones. Puh! The blind horse
. . . the big toe . . .

LACHESIS:

The cloud . . . the eyelashes of Hera . . .

CLOTHO:

Harping on one string.
What is it that first goes on four legs . . .?

ATROPOS:

The porpoise . . . Etna . . .

APOLLO:

Everyone knows those! I have some new ones—

SISTERS:

Again, a scream.
New ones!

APOLLO:

Slowly.
What is it that is necessary to—
He pauses. The SISTERS *are riveted.*

LACHESIS:

Go on, boy, go on. What is it that is necessary to—

APOLLO:

But—I only play for forfeits. See! If I lose . . .

CLOTHO:

If you looth, you mutht tell uth which one ith the faireth.

APOLLO:

No! No! I dare not!

LACHESIS:

    Sharply.

Yes!

APOLLO:

And if I win?

ATROPOS:

Win? Idiot! Stupid! Slave! No one has ever won from us.

APOLLO:

But if I win?

LACHESIS:

He doesn't know who we are!

APOLLO:

But if I win?

CLOTHO:

The fool talkth of winning!

APOLLO:

If I win, you must grant me one wish. One wish, any wish.

LACHESIS:

Yes, yes. Oh, what a tedious fellow! Go on with your riddle. What is it that is necessary to—

APOLLO:

Swear by Acheron!

CLOTHO and LACHESIS:

We swear! By Acheron! By Acheron!

APOLLO:

    To ATROPOS.

You, too.

ATROPOS:

> *After a moment's brooding resistance, loudly.*

By Acheron!

APOLLO:

Then: ready?

LACHESIS:

Wait! One moment.

> *Leaning toward* ATROPOS, *confidentially.*

The sun is near setting. Do not forget the thread of Ad—You know, the thread of Ad—

ATROPOS:

What? What Ad? What are you whispering about, silly?

LACHESIS:

> *Somewhat louder.*

Not to forget the thread of Admetus, King of Thessaly. At sundown. Have you lost your shears, Atropos?

ATROPOS:

Oh, stop your buzzing and fussing and tend to your own business. Of course I haven't lost my shears. Go on with your riddle, boy!

APOLLO:

So! I'll give you as much time as it takes to recite the names of the Muses and their mother.

LACHESIS:

Hm! Nine and one. Well, begin!

APOLLO:

What is it that is necessary to every life—and that can save only one?

The SISTERS *rock back and forth with closed eyes, mumbling the words of the riddle. Suddenly* APOLLO *starts singing his invocation to the Muses.*

> Mnemosyne, mother of the nine;
> Polyhymnia, incense of the gods—

LACHESIS:

> *Shrieks.*

Don't sing! Unfair! How can we think?

CLOTHO:

Stop your ears, sister.

ATROPOS:

Unfair!

> *Murmuring.*

What is it that can save every life—

> *They put their fingers in their ears.*

APOLLO:

Erato, voice of love;
Euterpe, help me now.

Calliope, thief of our souls;
Urania, clothed of the stars;
Clio of the backward glances;
Euterpe, help me now.

Terpsichore of the beautiful ankles;
Thalia of long laughter;
Melpomene, dreaded and welcome;
Euterpe, help me now.

> *Then, in a loud voice.*

Forfeit! Forfeit!

126

CLOTHO *and* ATROPOS *bury their faces in* LACHESIS'S *neck, moaning.*

LACHESIS:
> *In a dying voice.*

What is the answer?

APOLLO:
> *Flinging away his hat, triumphantly.*

Myself! Apollo the sun.

SISTERS:

Apollo! You?

LACHESIS:
> *Savagely.*

Pah! What life can you save?

APOLLO:

My forfeit! One wish! One life! The life of Admetus, King of Thessaly.
> *A horrified clamor arises from the* SISTERS.

SISTERS:

Fraud! Impossible! Not to be thought of!

APOLLO:

By Acheron.

SISTERS:

Against all law. Zeus will judge. Fraud.

APOLLO:
> *Warning.*

By Acheron.

SISTERS:

Zeus! We will go to Zeus about it. He will decide.

APOLLO:

Zeus swears by Acheron and keeps his oath.
> *Sudden silence.*

ATROPOS:

> *Decisive but ominous.*

You will have your wish—the life of King Admetus. But—

APOLLO:

> *Triumphantly.*

I shall have the life of Admetus!

SISTERS:

But—

APOLLO:

I shall have the life of Admetus! What is your *but?*

ATROPOS:

Someone else must die in his stead.

APOLLO:

> *Lightly.*

Oh—choose some slave. Some gray and greasy thread on your lap, divine Lachesis.

LACHESIS:

> *Outraged.*

What? You ask me to take a life?

ATROPOS:

You ask us to murder?

CLOTHO:

Apollo thinks that we are criminals?

APOLLO:
> *Beginning to be fearful.*

Then, great sisters, how is this to be done?

LACHESIS:

Me—an assassin?
> *She spreads her arms wide and says solemnly:*

Over my left hand is Chance; over my right hand is Necessity.

APOLLO:

Then, gracious sisters, how will this be done?

LACHESIS:

Someone must *give* his life for Admetus—of free choice and will. Over such deaths we have no control. Neither Chance nor Necessity rules the free offering of the will. Someone must choose to die in the place of Admetus, King of Thessaly.

APOLLO:
> *Covering his face with his hands.*

No! No! I see it all!
> *With a loud cry.*

Alcestis! Alcestis!
> *And he runs stumbling from the scene.*

CURTAIN

E40863

PS3545
.I345A78 Wilder, Thornton Niven, 1897-1975.   8.95
        The Alcestiad; or, A life in the sun; a
     play in three acts; with a satyr play, The
     drunken sisters.   New York, Harper & Row
     [c1977]
        129 p.   ∂ 7/94
        "A Cass Canfield book."   3-12/08

        1. Alcestis-Drama.   I. Wilder, Thornton
     Niven, 1897-1975.   The drunken sisters.
     II. Title.   III. Title: The drunken sisters.
     IV. Title: A life   in the sun.
                                   77-3781